STRIPED BASS FISHING

Secrets of Striped Bass Fishing

by D.W. Bennett

ISBN 0-88839-103-X

Copyright © 1982 D.W. Bennett

Cataloging in Publication Data.

Bennett, D.W.
  Secrets of striped bass fishing
  (Northeast fishing series)
 	
  1. Striped bass fishing. 2. Striped bass. I. Title.
  II. Series.
  SH691.S7B4   799.1'758   C81-091101-9

All rights reserved. No part of this publication may be reproduced, stored in a retrieval system or transmitted, in any form or by any means, electronic, mechanical, photocopying, recording or otherwise, without the prior written permission of Hancock House Publishers.

Editor Margaret Campbell
Typeset by Anne Whatcott in Garamond type on an AM Varityper Comp/Edit
Layout Linda Rourke
Production & Cover Design Peter Burakoff
Artwork by Barb Wood
Printed by Friesen Printers, Altona, Manitoba, Canada
Front Cover Photo: Al Ristori
Back Cover Photos (Top): Spider Andresen
            (Bottom): Dery W. Bennett

Hancock House Publishers
256 Route 81, Killingworth, CT, U.S.A. 06417
Hancock House Publishers Ltd.
19313 Zero Avenue, Surrey, B.C., Canada V3S 5J9

Table of Contents

Acknowledgments and Dedication 4
    About Striped Bass 6
1. Habits of Striped Bass 14
2. Stripers in the Surf 29
3. Other Shore Fishing 58
4. Fishing for Stripers from Boats 61
5. The Future of the Striped Bass 74
6. Caring for, Cleaning and Cooking Your Catch 76

Acknowledgments and Dedication

Many good striped bass fishermen have shared their secrets and their enthusiasms: Jimmy Cousins, Wally Smith, and Bob Lick in New Jersey; Appy Middleton and Ned Gerber in the Chesapeake; Al Ristori in New York Harbor; Larry Kabat on some New England shores; and a stranger on Cape Cod who once shared his fishing gear with me when I was weaponless and bass were tearing up the surf.

I have picked the brains of Bob Boyle, Bob Pond, Bruce Freeman, Pete Barrett, Ben Florence, and John Clark.

The painstaking record keeping of Graham Macmillan and Mary Ann Griesbach, who conduct the American Littoral Society's tagging program, has provided glimpses of bass migrations. And what striped bass fanatic cannot benefit as I have from dipping into the writings of Nelson Bryant, George Reiger, Nicholas Karas, and Frank Moss?

My father shares much of the credit and none of the blame, for he took me out fishing a long time ago thinking it a worthy venture. I took him at his word.

Author's Note

I saw my first striped bass when I was about twelve years old. It was a small fish, caught in a gill net on the Corsica River on Maryland's Eastern Shore. I was helping a local fisherman catch hardheads (croakers) for market. I recall that while we picked the hardheads and tossed them into baskets, he put the striper carefully into a bucket, saying it was going not to market but into his frying pan that evening. Hardheads for the folks at the store, stripers for home consumption.

I thought the striper was only a very large striped mullet, and I said so.

"That's right boy," he answered, a little meanly. "And you just keep on thinking that. And anytime you get one of these 'mullet' you just give it to me and I'll take care of it."

That was the first time I had an inkling that striped bass were something special.

Secrets of Striped Bass Fishing

About Striped Bass

Striped Bass *(Morone saxatilis)* are probably the most sought after inshore gamefish of the mid-Atlantic coast. Certainly these fish attract more serious sportsfishermen and more newspaper and magazine coverage than any other fish, as well as more angling theories, both true and false.

Striped bass can be caught 100 miles upriver from salt water, they can be caught on mud flats, and they can be trolled or jigged up from sixty feet. They are in the St. Lawrence River, they are found off Cape Cod, they throng in the Hudson and Chesapeake, in the Cooper-Santee freshwater impoundment system, and in rivers of the Carolinas. Another large group populates the west coast, from California almost to the Canadian border. There is a similar species in the Mediterranean. But here our subject is the Atlantic Coast striper, found mostly from Massachusetts to Chesapeake Bay.

These magnificent fish can be caught in the middle of the night in the surf on lures, at midday on cut bait, during storms when it is almost impossible to cast, and by deep trolling big spoons and natural baits. They may also refuse to be caught in any of those places or those conditions. There are fishermen who have managed to *not* catch striped bass for months and even years. But persist. One day you'll succeed and the fish you catch will be lovely and strong, with flashing scales, bold dark stripes, a broad tail, wide shoulders: a fish of clear eye and noble spirit.

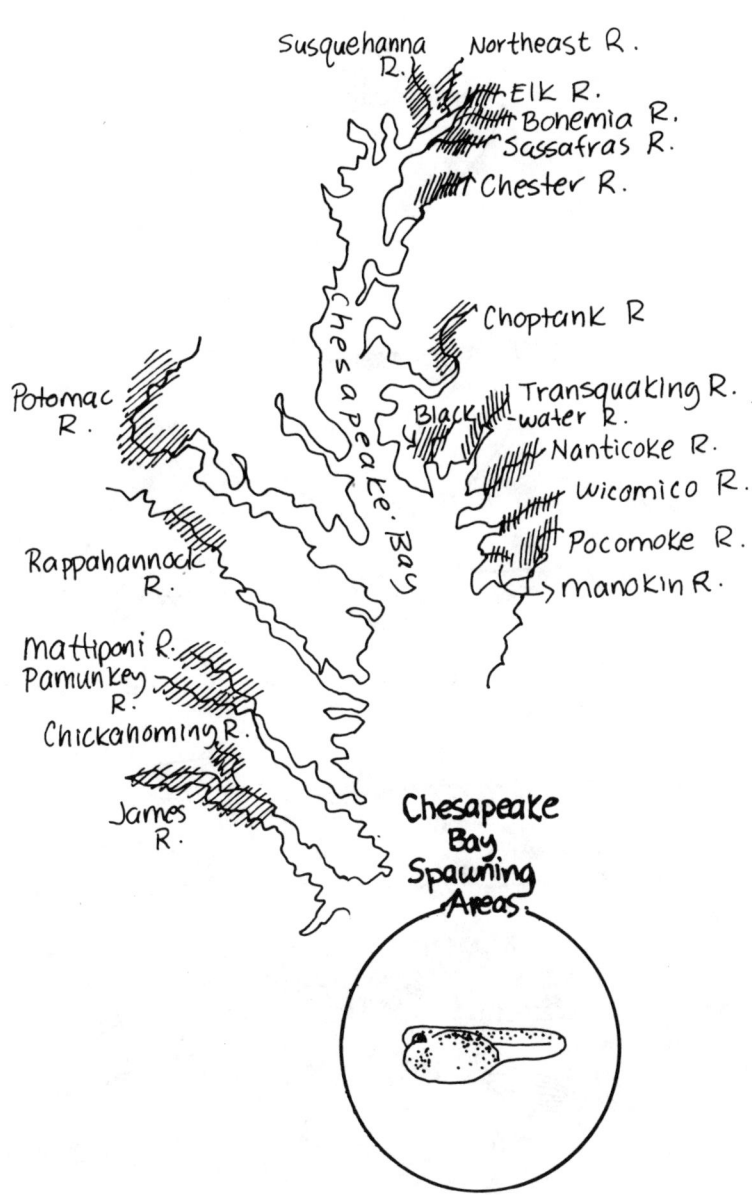

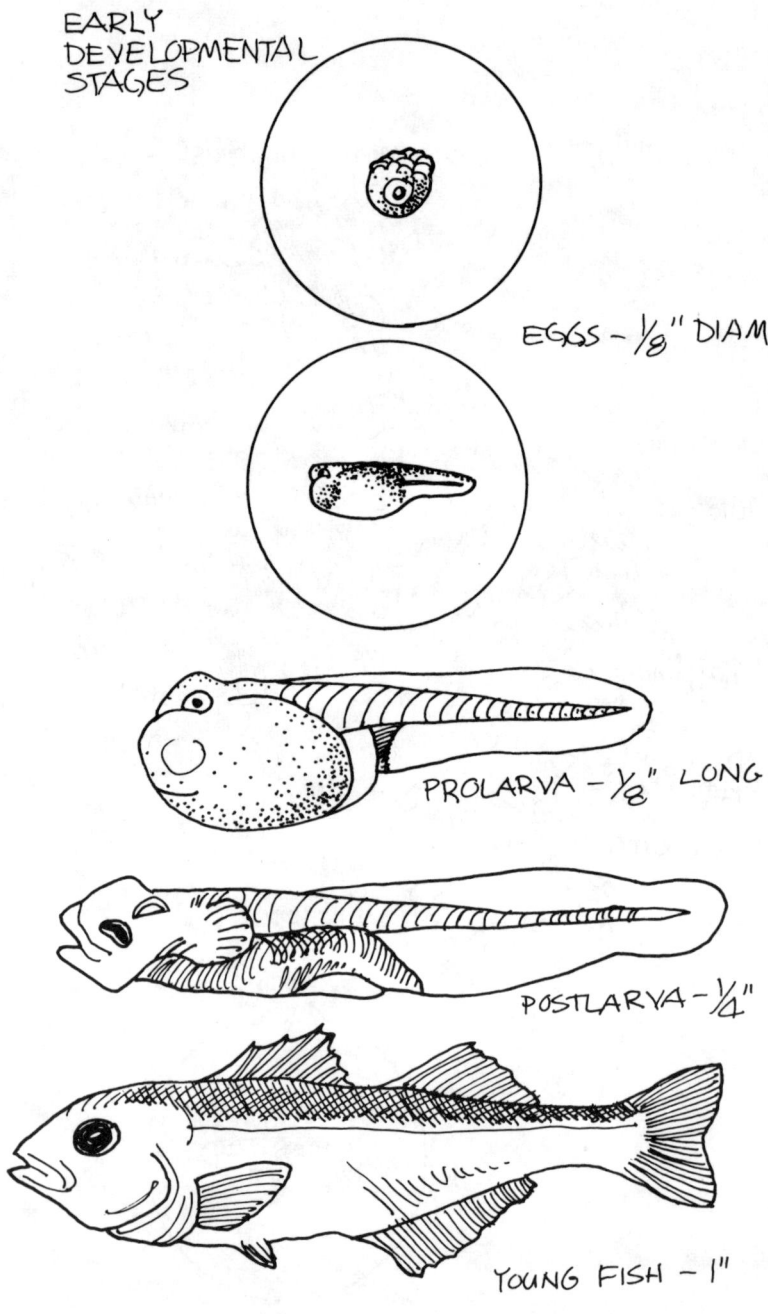

From Cradle to Grave

Striped bass hatch in the spring from eggs cast in two major estuaries of the northeast, the Hudson River, and stretches of rivers emptying into Chesapeake Bay. Striped bass are anadromous, that is, they mature at sea, but run into fresh water to spawn. One special exception is worth noting here: the Chesapeake-Delaware Canal is now a major breeding location. The eggs are spawned very near where rivers change from salt to fresh. That means up the Hudson as far as West Point, some eighty miles from the sea; and in the Chesapeake area, up the Potomac as far as seventy miles from the bay proper and about fifty miles from the ocean waters east of the Chesapeake Bay Bridge Tunnel, between Cape Charles and Norfolk. The preferred water temperature for spawning and hatching is about 45 degrees F. The eggs hatch in about three days and for several days, the larvae drift with the currents and tides and live off the food supply of the yolk sac. Within two weeks of hatching, the fish are a quarter of an inch long and have begun to feed actively on small plankton. They gradually progress to larger fare—small fish, shrimps. In some rivers, insects make up a major proportion of the diet. At the end of their first summer, stripers are about an inch long.

Striped bass appear to spend about two years in their natal streams and bays, and then join an awe-inspiring migration ritual. They move in schools to the sea and north in late spring, returning southward in the fall to winter in the deeper waters of rivers and bays. Most of them return to their birthplaces, but there are, as always, exceptions. Some bass are born in one river or stream, but return to another. A large number of fish, many of them weighing fifteen pounds or more, winter off the Carolina Capes, and some very large fish have been found wintering in small rivers in Maine and further south.

Striped bass usually travel in large schools when they are small, up to ten pounds or so. Then the school size decreases. Large striped bass—twenty-five pounds or more—seem to be loners, except during spawning runs.

Striped bass are active, aggressive predators. Among their favorite foods are worms, crabs, squid, shrimp, and a large number of fish, notably eels, bunker, mackerel, anchovy, silversides, sand eels, and various bottom fish.

Striped bass grow to great size. Several of more than 100 pounds in weight having been reported by commercial fishermen in North Carolina. However, the recognized world record fish is one of seventy-three pounds caught off Cuttyhunk, Massachusetts, in June of 1967.

Fish are about five inches long at the end of their first year, and twelve inches long at two years. The average length and weight of striped bass at different ages is well shown in this chart, done by Alice Jane Mansueti:

AVERAGE LENGTH AND WEIGHT OF STRIPED BASS AT DIFFERENT AGES.

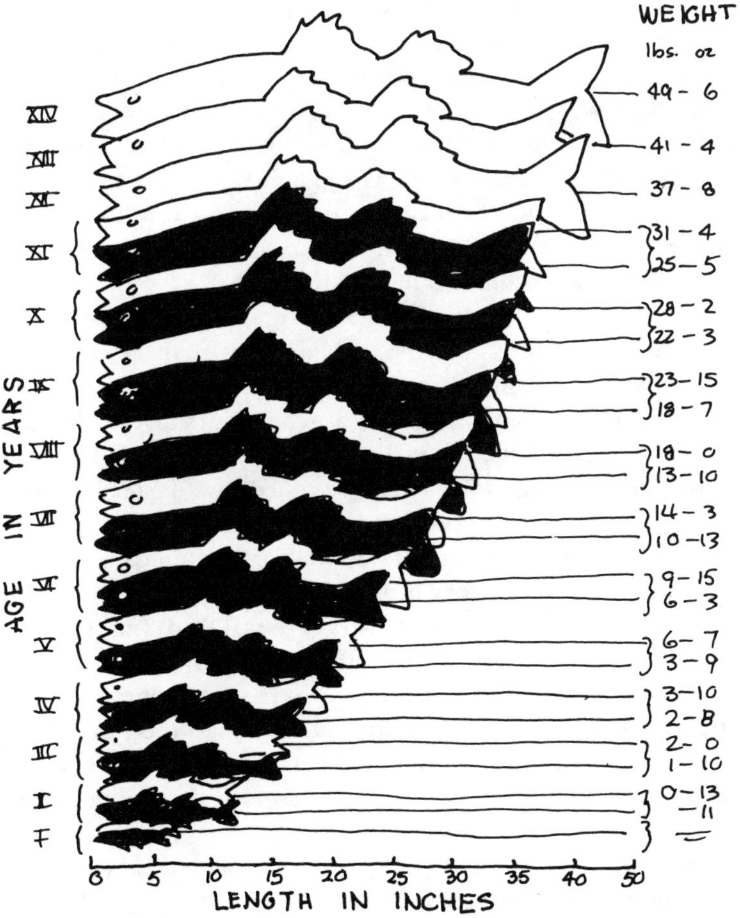

Age (Years)	Weight (lbs. oz)
XIV	49 – 6
XIII	41 – 4
XII	37 – 8
XI	31 – 4 / 25 – 5
X	28 – 2 / 22 – 3
IX	23 – 15 / 18 – 7
VIII	18 – 0 / 13 – 10
VII	14 – 3 / 10 – 13
VI	9 – 15 / 6 – 3
V	6 – 7 / 3 – 9
IV	3 – 10 / 2 – 8
III	2 – 0 / 1 – 10
I	0 – 13 / – 11
F	

LENGTH IN INCHES (0–50)

female / ← FORK LENGTH / male

Note that above twenty-five pounds, the chart shows no male bass. This is generally true, although males have been found as large as thirty-two pounds. The fact remains, almost any bass you catch over twenty-five pounds and longer than forty inches will be a female.

These females are prodigious egg layers. It is estimated that a female bass will carry as many as 100,000 eggs per pound of body weight. Thus, a fifty-pound female can lay as many as 5,000,000 eggs. During spawning, she will be accompanied by as many as a dozen smaller males—five to ten pounds—who crowd the female and spread their milt as she lays eggs. The commotion that this spawning-fertilization activity can cause in shallow water is called a rock fight in the Chesapeake—which brings us to the various names for this mighty fish.

In the northeast, from Canada south, it is called the striped bass, or striper for short. From Delaware south, it is usually called rockfish, or just plain rock (hence, rock fight). Small fish are sometimes called school bass or schoolies (shorts if they are below the legal limit), and really large ones can be called lunkers or bull bass (though they should be called cows instead of bulls above the twenty-five pound range).

Whatever the name, stripers are well-proportioned, well-built fish, with large, hard broad heads, muscular shoulders and backs, and broad tails. They have two sets of dorsal (top) fins, the first with from seven to nine sharp spines, the second with twelve to fourteen softer rays. Stripers usually have seven unbroken black stripes down their silvery white sides, though the stripes can sometimes be slightly broken. From above, the bass appears to be dark greenish, from the side light gray with black stripes. The belly is white.

The mouth has thick tough lips, but, although it is a predator, it has no visible, sharp teeth. It tends to grab its prey and either crush it or swallow it whole.

Biologists have been able to cross striped bass with the freshwater white bass, coming up with what could be considered either a stunted striper or a huge white bass, up to twelve pounds and two feet. Land-locked bass in the Cooper-Santee reservoir system in South Carolina reach forty pounds.

EXTERNAL ANATOMY OF THE STRIPED BASS

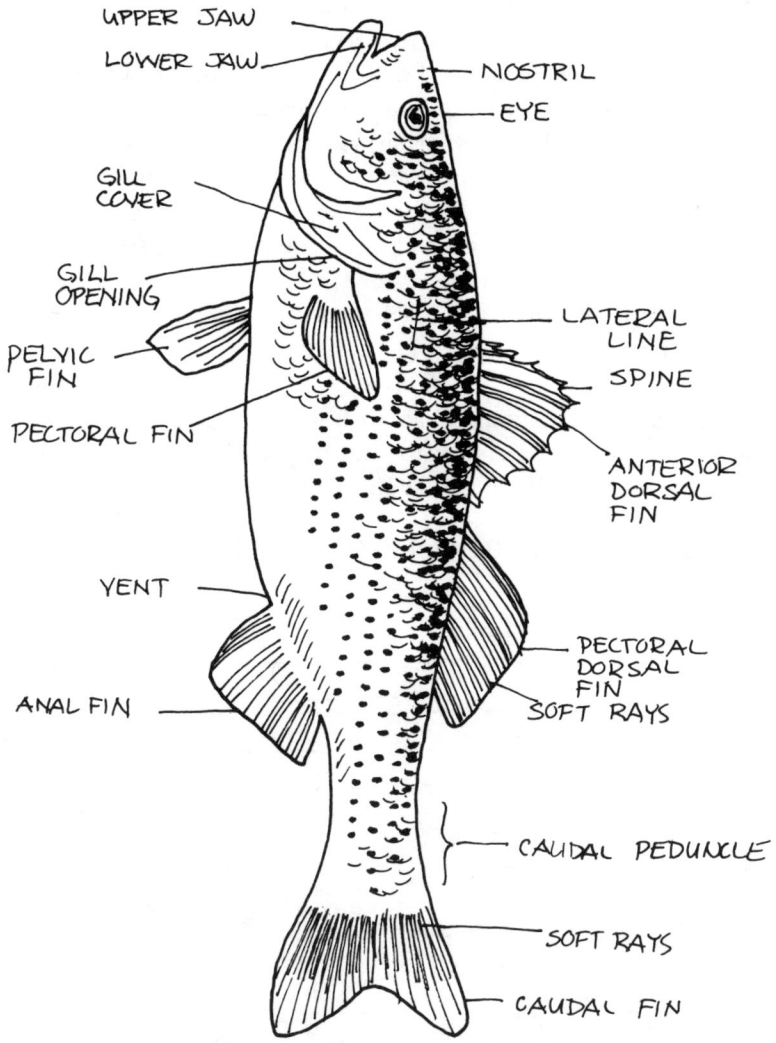

1. HABITS OF STRIPED BASS

If you are after a species of fish, it is valuable to learn about the fish. This will help you figure out where bass might be and what will attract them. It is useful, however, to remember that fish behavior can be consistent most of the time but vary just enough to make the exception worth worrying about also. To cite one example, striped bass are known to favor rough water and moving tides, and they are thought to avoid the bright light of a noonday sun, but I know a serious striper fisherman who likes to walk the beaches near his place of work during lunch hour, casting a small surface lure into the surf as he walks. On a white hot August noon, with nary a breeze (he recalls the flies on the beach were fierce), he cast his lure into an utterly still, shallow surf and caught a fifteen pound bass, a fish he thought so perfect in proportion and markings that he had it mounted. It shouldn't have happened, but it did. Having said all that, however, here are some general thoughts about how striped bass act. These guidelines should lead you to the proper place to fish at the proper time with the proper bait.

Striped bass and temperature

Stripers are less active in water temperatures below forty degrees and above seventy-five degrees. They are most active—moving and feeding—when the temperature is between fifty-five and sixty-five degrees. Thus, a first rule: fish for striped bass from mid-spring to late fall, but, if you live in an area where sea temperatures get into the mid-seventies, expect fishing to slow down. Look then for cooler water. Often this means fishing in deeper water or on the bottom.

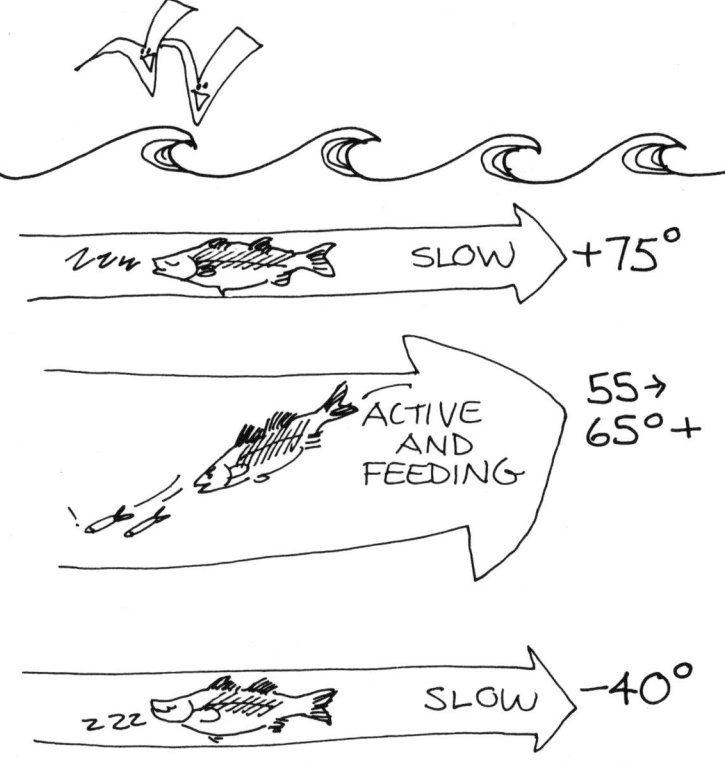

At temperatures below forty degrees, the striped bass are inactive. As temperatures drop in the fall, they move toward warmer waters, either to the south, or offshore and deep, or upstream into deep pockets in bays and rivers. This striped bass habit became well known to New Jersey anglers when the Garden State Parkway was built after World War II, a construction project that led to the dredging of a deep hole in the Mullica River. Striped bass poured into this hole in the fall, there to wait out the winter. Water temperatures froze the river's surface while the fish lay dormant forty feet below in the "Garden State Parkway Hole." Fishermen went out onto the ice, cut holes in it, and jigged bare treble hooks down to the bottom, snagging many bass until the State closed the striped bass season from December 31 to March 31, to protect this stationary, vulnerable population.

In another spot, biologists dragging nets in the upper Hudson River during the winter of 1967 managed to fill a net so full they could hardly pull it aboard—striped bass up to forty pounds, again wintering over in a deep river hole.

Striped bass and season

Water temperature and season are, of course, related. At the beginning of the year, bass are bedded for winter, maybe up a Rhode Island or Delaware river, but most probably in the Hudson River, in the lower end of Chesapeake Bay, or in the ocean slightly offshore from southern New Jersey to Cape Hatteras. In many places, these bass are within a narrow temperature range, say thirty-three to forty degrees. Below that temperature they freeze to death; above that temperature, they are too active to be dormant and must feed themselves at a time when food is scarce. You can imagine bass at this time of year, hovering between sleep and wakefulness, barely moving, keeping away from strong currents, their gills pumping just enough to keep low levels of oxygen coursing through their circulatory systems.

As the temperature rises, the fish stir. At forty-five degrees, they will begin to move and feed lightly. Their movements will be local. If the temperature drops, they drop back to dormancy. Temperatures rise again, bass move and feed, ever more and faster as the waters warm. This is about mid-April along the Maryland/Delaware/New Jersey shore, a few weeks later to the north. At about this time, two kinds of migrations begin. One is made up of fish that have wintered offshore. They move inshore and north, feeding as they go. This means the beginning of fishing for stripers in the surf and in boats near shore. This migration and feeding peaks in June. By late June or July, these bass populations have ended their migrations north. Some have settled down for summer feeding.

Another migration starts up rivers for spawning. From the lower Chesapeake, fish move boldly into Nanticoke, the Potomac, the James, the York, and the Rappahannock, and into the Chesapeake and Delaware Canal. After spawning, these fish move downstream and spread generally around the Bay. Fish that have wintered in the Hudson move upriver to near West Point to spawn and then drop downriver and out of the Hudson into New York Harbor, up along the south shore of Long Island, into Long Island Sound, and around Sandy Hook and about fifteen to thirty miles south. They will move into the mouths of many rivers in Long Island Sound, feeding heavily.

By mid-summer, striped bass are spread broadly through their range. At this time, bass tend to be alone or in small groups rather than in schools. The first hints of fall change this pattern. For one thing, other fish begin to school for southern movements. Mullet, menhaden, mackerel, and other species gather to move. Striped bass begin to gather too, and by September the first schools of fish are moving south from Cape Cod, although striped bass are still caught there in November. The main body of fish, however, has passed Montauk, on the eastern end of Long Island, by October and has passed down and off the New Jersey coast by early November. But—mark it well—striped bass can still be caught in the nearshore waters around Thanksgiving.

Another fall migration brings striped bass from the ocean upriver. Sometimes these are small fish. It is well known, for example, that Brooklyn piers are hot spots for short bass in November. Fish around nine to fifteen inches can be found among the piers by the thousands, feeding on silversides and shrimp before heading up into the Hudson for the winter.

During these fall movements, striped bass are hungry, building their fat for winter. All in all, fall is the best time to catch bass.

But again, the exceptions: in parts of the Chesapeake, small bass can be caught almost all winter, and they continue to be active feeders in the warm water discharges of power and sewer plants, although the surroundings might not be the most pleasant for fishermen.

After this last flurry of fall, striped bass disappear from the seascape. But in spring, when water temperatures begin to rise, the fish will start the cycle again.

Striped bass and light

Striped bass can see at night, they feed at night, and they can be caught at night. The same three things can be said about striped bass during the day. Divers exploring jetties off New York have seen bass during the daytime moving slowly, close to the jetty rocks, doing nothing but keeping a little water going over their gills. The same divers at night have seen bass foraging on the bottom for crabs, yet at other times lying almost dormant.

NIGHT FEEDERS!

It appears that striped bass have a keen sense of smell and use this sense to locate food. It also seems that striped bass have good, close-up eyesight, and that they feed, or at least strike or lunge for food, by sight. They also have a good sense of hearing. And, like most fish, they have pressure-sensitive organs along the sides of their bodies which enable them to detect water movement.

All of this means that you can fish for striped bass at any stage of sunlight or darkness. It is possible to talk to striped bass fishermen who fish almost exclusively at night; others stick with daytime fishing, and still others are most fond of the early morning and late afternoon hours.

Striped bass can be active during any of the twenty-four hours in a day and they feed whenever food is around to attract them and trigger feeding behavior.

Striped bass and water movement

Striped bass are strong fish and can cope with the stress of heavy wave and tide action. They are muscular in the shoulders with broad powerful tails connected to the body by a beefy peduncle. They are not quick like a defensive halfback nor are they stolid like a defensive tackle: they are like linebackers, strong and fairly fast.

Striped bass can move right into a surf breaker line and handle themselves with ease. They can hug a wave-struck jetty and still feed. They can hang in a strong undertow and dig out crabs. And they can hunker in behind bridge abutments and then move out into six-knot currents to pick off swimming worms and fish. Sometimes, when feeding most recklessly, they follow bait up through the surf onto the beach, and then they have to struggle back into the sea on their sides, but they can do this without missing a beat.

All things being equal, striped bass tend to feed more aggressively when a heavy sea or surf or tide is running, as if they can handle the elements better than their prey. They are not afraid to be abroad in a storm, so the striped bass fishermen must not be afraid either.

Striped bass and birds

Surface feeding or moving bass are often accompanied by sea birds alert to feed on bait driven up to the surface. Two types are the most common over bass: laughing gulls and terns. Birds in a screaming horde usually mean fish.

Striped bass and food

Striped bass, like most fish, move for four basic reasons: to spawn, to migrate (sometimes combined), to eat or to avoid being eaten. The only times they apparently do not feed are when they are full of food or dormant in winter, and immediately before, during, and after spawning. At all other times, it is safe to say that a striped bass is actively interested in finding something to eat.

Striped bass have no single favorite food, but some generalizations can be made. In rivers, where most of the feeding bass are small—up to fifteen pounds—top choices are marine worms, crustaceans, and small fish. Larger fish and offshore fish go for the same foods, but add squid, lobster, and larger fish—menhaden, whiting, bluefish, weakfish, flatfish, spot, butterfish, and mackerel. They love eels, and they can and will crush and eat large crabs and small clams.

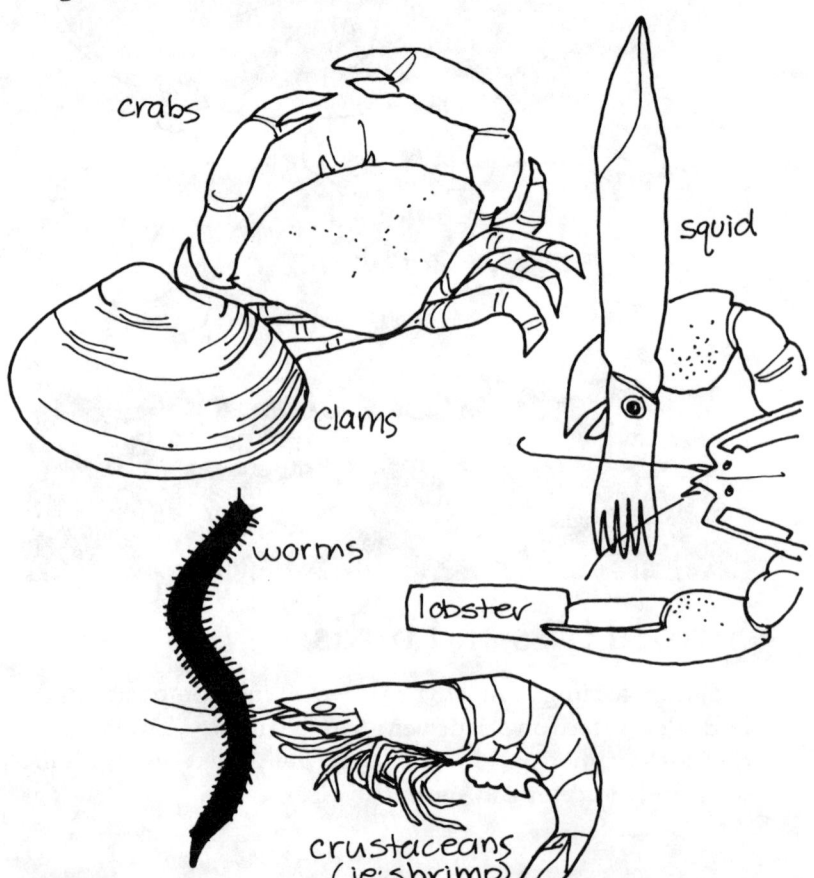

BAIT:

23

It is also well known that bass will sometimes choose to feed on one species to the exclusion of all else. Sometimes large bass will feed only on tiny anchovies, little two-inch fish. At other times, with schools of anchovies and silversides flashing at the surface, striped bass will choose to hug the bottom, feeding on crabs.

Out at sea a bit, stripers surrounded by schools of menhaden, may choose to strike at rigged eels. Or they will strike at bunker spoons, but not hit rigged live bunker. Striped bass can be caught with worm baits when no worms are around naturally, and they can be attracted to a lively popping surface lure when no bait is on the surface. They can be caught on large chunks of surf clam, which is not one of their natural foods.

Striped bass tend to feed heavily and then stop, as if to digest the contents of a full belly. Sometimes they will start feeding and stop almost immediately. A school will charge into baitfish, feed in thrashing abandon for, say, ten minutes, and then stop feeding in the blink of an eye.

There is one more important thing to know about bass: *they are repeaters*. They tend to repeat their movements and behavior from year to year, season to season, and from one day through night and into the next. This is the most important fact about striped bass that you should understand. Let me give some examples.

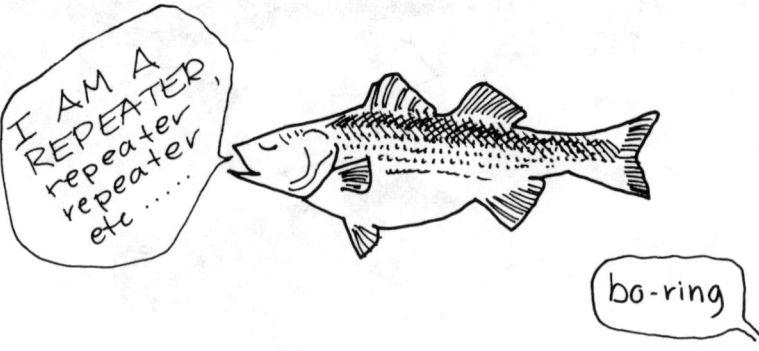

A huge volunteer effort among the members of the American Littoral Society has resulted in a major tagging program—140,000 tags out in its first fifteen years of operation. Many of those tags have been placed on striped bass, primarily fish from the eastern end of Cape Cod through to a few Chesapeake rivers. Thousands and thousands of striped bass, from fingerlings to fifty-pounders, have been caught, tagged, and released, and about 5% of these tagged fish have been recaptured. The Society has reams of return data, information on where these fish moved, and how fast they grew. Here are a few points that these returns show:

—Many striped bass are recaptured within miles of where they were tagged a year or more before, many within the same estuarine area. This is especially true of fish in the Lower Hudson River/New York Harbor area. Fish tagged on Staten Island's eastern shore are often recaptured there a year or two later. Long Island Sound bass are notorious for coming back to the same river mouth. The pattern, while not all-inclusive, is clear enough to indicate that a fisherman who catches striped bass at the mouth of the Connecticut River one fall, will catch them there also the next fall, either the same fish, fish from the same school, or later progeny of the original fish.

—Striped bass are caught not only in the same place, but also at the same time of the year, often the same day. There are enough instances of fish being caught exactly one year later to lead me to urge fishermen to go back on a strict schedule to places where fish were caught. If you caught bass on September 22 at the mouth of the Housatantic River this year, go back there next year, same time, same place. I'd even suggest you use the same bait or lure.

—Bass move with temperature. Littoral Society returns record waves of striped bass movement beginning with the early catches in the Chesapeake Bay areas in early March, followed by catches in New Jersey's Mullica River, then Long Island, and then Cape Cod. These tag returns reflect the movement of warmer temperatures toward the north. So watch sea temperatures closely. If, for example, the winter is warm and temperature holds up in spring, start your striped bass fishing excursions a little early.

Now, naturally, these three suggestions—fish the same place, same day, and watch temperature—are subject to all sorts of variations: tide, moon, storms, heavy rains and the subsequent runoff and changes in water quality, and untoward events like plankton blooms or explosions of baitfish like sand lance. It is these variations that make any fishing more fun. They add the fondly remembered twists—like the time in late fall when the surf is crashing and the snow is falling but you catch large bass when no respectable fish or fisherman should be abroad.

The best way to recall this information is to keep a fishing diary or log, and I recommend such record keeping to any fisherman who wants to catch more fish and have more fun doing it. I have found that pocket-sized five-year diaries are the best. In this way, you can see on each page five years of records. I usually note temperature, weather, and where I fish, using what lures or bait, tide and what happened. I will also make a note if I hear something about fish somewhere else, and, if I have room and energy, I will drop in general natural observations, such things as birds moving, bait around, other fish. I now have a handful of these little diaries (I once bought half a dozen of them when I found the right size), and they're worth an evening of review every once in a while. Here are two entries:

May 18: Watch Hill, R.I., 50 degrees and blowing hard from north. Fished rocks north of town at dawn. No action, but guy next to me hung big bass on popper, lost it. Fish reported on Nantucket, Vineyard.

August 16: Another try at slough on Sandy Hook. School bass still there. Six in twenty-five minutes, all on Hopkins. The fish are here same time, same tide, still feeding on crabs but hitting lures. Sunny and warm.

I believe that a successful fisherman is one who learns as much as possible about his quarry to the point where he is making a real effort to get right into the fish's head. This knowledge helps in two ways: first, the more you know about a fish, the more likely you are to be successful catching it. Second, most successful fishermen work (or at least play) the game hard. They concentrate on fishing and they fish with confidence. Most good fishermen I know go fishing with a firm belief in success. They KNOW they are going to catch striped bass. And very often they do.

One point to note, though: travel light, at least at the beginning. Heaven knows, striped bass fishermen are unsurpassed in their willingness to load up with extra bits of gear that will do everything from aim the cast to measure the captured fish's every dimension. I suggest instead that you start with the essentials and then add grudgingly as you learn.

One final note: when in doubt, go fishing. If you have two hours to kill, head for striped bass. Don't stay home and decide the wind isn't quite right or the tide is too low or your back hurts. Go after striped bass, because one time, you'll stay home and the guy down the street won't, and he'll come back with a bunch of fish and you'll kick your theories, your diaries, and yourself from here to there.

2. STRIPERS IN THE SURF

Striped bass can be caught in the surf from Cape Cod to Cape Henlopen from April to November, but the spring run at the south end of this range is short and sweet. Best summer striped bass fishing in the surf is from Atlantic City north, better by night than by day, and better as the season progresses. The best time is from mid-September or until it's too cold for either fish or man.

Surf-fishing means standing at the ocean's edge and casting bait or lure to where you think the fish are. So you need to make decisions about where to fish and when, about tackle and casting technique, and about bait or lure. Much of what is said here applies to other striped bass fishing methods also.

Where to fish

It is important to understand beaches and surf, to begin to know why and how surf water moves, where bars form and how they affect water movement, and how tides change water movement.

So, let's start on a beach at low tide and watch it and the water through one six-hour cycle, from low to high. Say that our visit is at a time when there have been no recent storms and when there is no significant wind. Stand at the water's edge and look out to sea.

Right in front of you and out about twenty-five to fifty yards is still water, maybe up to four feet deep. Then the water color changes, get less dark, and small waves are forming. This is a sandbar. It might have just several inches of water covering it, or, in some cases, it might be dry. Now, let's wade out and climb onto the bar. Beyond, the water deepens gradually. If you stand on the bar and wait about an hour, you will feel the water deepening. A slight rush of water will push landward. The tide is coming in. In two hours, it might rise a foot or so. The waves

"Scouring"

Dropoff — *Inner bar* — *Outer bar*

(Enlargement of above)

The force of a wave rushing up the beach and then back to sea has a scouring or digging effect on the area immediately in the wash.

on the bar will be higher and stronger. Behind you, in the water between the bar and the beach, a slight chop can be seen and waves are pushing up the beach. It's time to wade back across the water (called a slough or gully) and get back to the beach.

Once on the beach, turn around. As the water on the bar deepens, the waves out there die out. This is because waves need to "feel bottom" to break, and, on a gentle day, the bar will "disappear" as the tide comes in. The waves feel bottom only near the beach and wave heights increase as the tide comes in. By now the waves are rolling up the beach, and soon they reach the beach crest or berm, there to die, although one wave in a dozen might slurp up over the berm.

It is now about six hours later and the tide is high. Soon the waterline will start to recede and six hours later, things will be back the way they were when you first got to the beach. The tide cycle is complete and will start again. Actually, in most areas of the northeast, a cycle from low to high takes a little more than six hours. A handy rule of thumb is that one day's high tide will be about a hour later than the one the day before. And it works out. Tides react to phases of the moon and every twenty-eight days, the tide will be high at almost exactly the same time.

Already, on this simplified beach, some guidelines for surf fishing can be set. At dead low tide, under the above weather conditions, the best approach to fishing this beach would be to wade across the slough and stand on the bar, fishing the deeper water beyond the bar for an hour or so. Then, as the water on the bar deepens, wade back across the slough and fish from the beach proper. When on the beach, try to reach the bar and fish on top of it, if you can cast that far. As the tide rises, stripers will often move onto the bar to feed. As you are driven back up the beach by deeper water, fish the slough, because now, as it has deepened, it becomes a collection place for bait, attracting stripers. If.you have arrived at the beach two hours after the tide has started in, fish the bar, if you can reach it, and the slough later. If you arrive two hours before low tide, fish the slough and the bar and then wade the slough and fish the surf beyond the bar just as soon as you can.

So much for a simplified beach. Now, let's add some complications or modifications, both natural and man-made. The tactics will change and they should change, especially to take advantage of these irregularities on the beach, for one of the first rules of surf-fishing for striped bass is to look for irregularities and fish those hardest.

That offshore bar I mentioned earlier is seldom one simple stretch of sand. Usually such a bar will have breaks in it. The water can rush in and out of the breaks, churning the water, gathering bait, and generally making for good fishing. So, one rule is always fish breaks in bars. At dead low tide, you can fish the outer part of these breaks. As the tide comes in and you are casting from the beach, cover these breaks and the waters near them. If they don't produce, then try something completely different. Ignore the breaks and fish the slough between the breaks. If stripers are avoiding the breaks, it may be because bait has gathered away from them. Keep in mind that if you are fishing a spot and not producing, you should change tactics. Conditions in tide waters are always changing, and the striped bass fisherman should be ready to change too.

Also, the offshore bar may extend 100 yards or so along a beach and then simply disappear. Bass can get in behind this sort of bar and set up feeding stations at either end. If the current is coming from your right to your left, the bass may be at the right hand end of the bar waiting for bait swept in behind the bar by the current, or they can be at the other end waiting for baitfish to be swept out from behind the bar. So fish the ends of bars also.

The beach itself might take a jog, or have a point, or there might be a cove cut back into the beach. These beach formations are caused by changes in offshore currents and any change in current is caused by a change in topography of either the bottom or the beach. So look for these irregularities and fish them.

Many beaches of the northeast have man-made structures thrusting out into the current, efforts to protect and build beaches. These rocks or pilings or wood bulkheads, called jetties or groins, are usually hot spots for striper fishing.

Any structure jutting out into the ocean changes currents and bottom topography. Usually, the upstream side of a groin has shoal water and there will be a gully or deep spot on the downstream side in behind the groin. Stripers tend to gather around these structures for several reasons. First, the marine growth on the rocks attracts small fish, prey for stripers. Also, baitfish will huddle in behind a groin to avoid a strong current. And crabs and bits of food also collect here. Bass are strong enough to hunker in against jetty rocks, so when you fish these areas, cover every inch of the jetty, from the end right to the base.

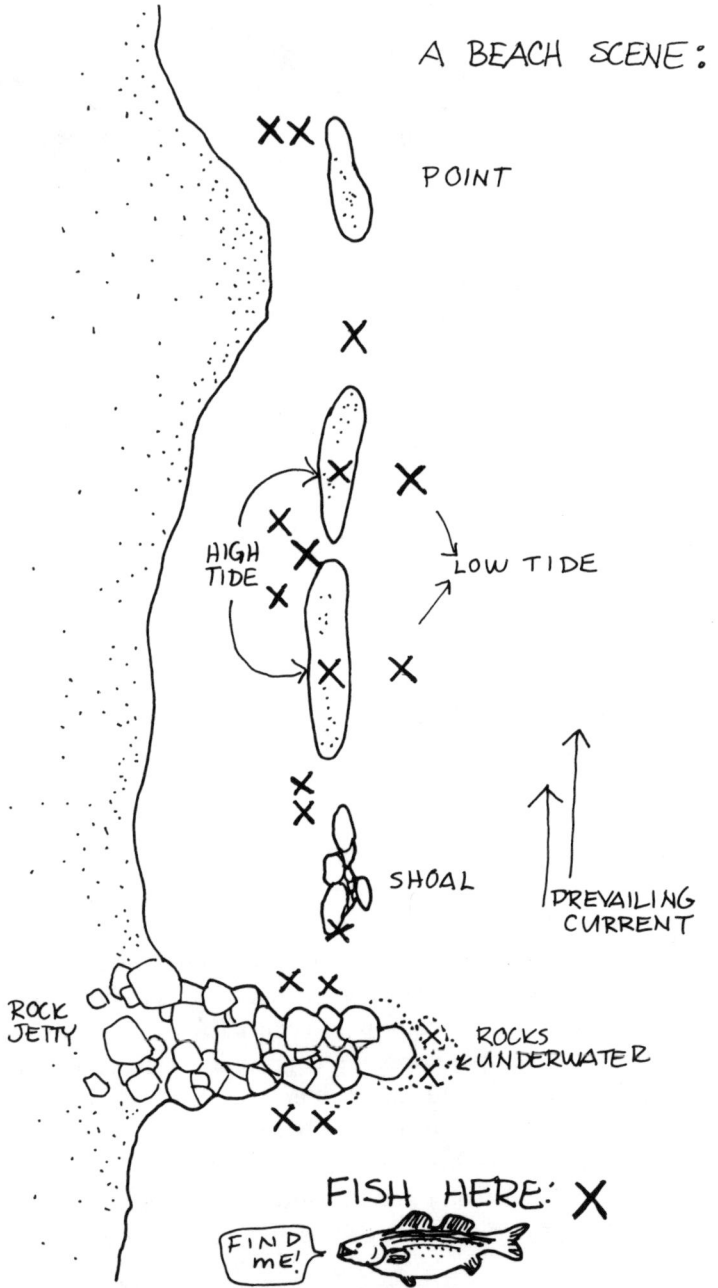

Winds, Storms, Tides, Currents

Back in our discussion of a typical beach, we assumed no winds or storms, but wind is a fact of life in the surf. Seldom is it windless. However, it is extremely difficult to know how wind conditions affect fishing. This set of one-liners about wind is fun to recite but dangerous to follow:

Wind from the north, don't venture forth.
Wind from the east, fishing least.
Wind from the south, blows the hook in the fish's mouth.
Wind from the west, fishing best.

Now, here are some facts: some of the best fall striped bass fishing is during the first part of a northeast storm, when winds are rising and the sea is beginning to churn. A west wind often drops surf water temperatures ten degrees in a tide, enough to move feeding fish offshore and off their feed. A south wind can bring warm dampness, muggy close hot weather and doldrums. And, finally, one of the best fall striped bass days I ever had was during the second day of a northeaster, with winds so strong I couldn't cast my favorite lures and was using an over-sized metal

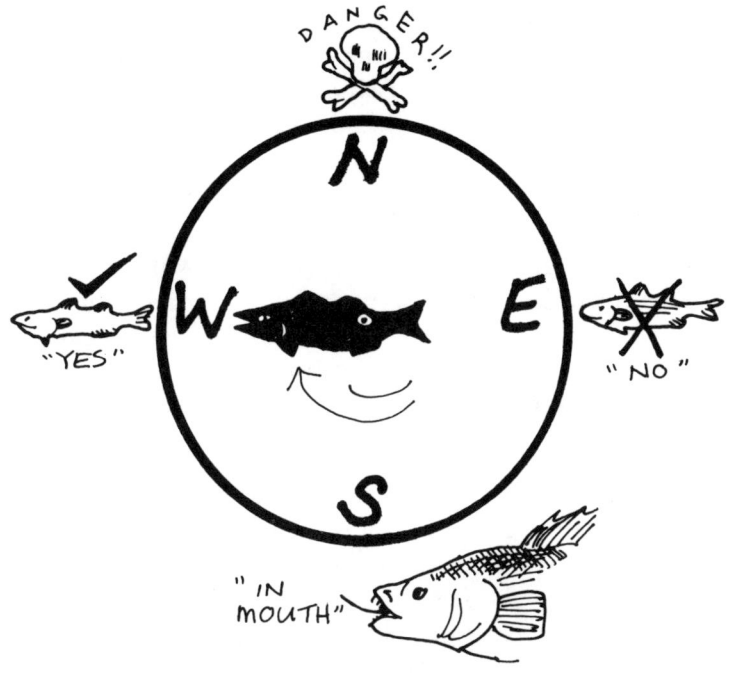

jig, and the ocean color was mud brown. Bass were breaking all one afternoon. Almost a hit every cast. So much for wind rules.

Most beaches, too, are subject to currents that carry water along the beach. Sometimes a storm or offshore event will send a swell in toward the beach, and of course the tide is always an effective water-moving agent. Take all these together and it is easy to understand that the surf moves in and out *and* up and down the beach. Notice how seldom waves come straight onto a beach. Usually they come in at an angle. An average wave comes from your right or left, washes up the beach behind you, and then runs down on your other side. That wave direction usually indicates the current along the shore. When you are fishing the surf with lures (see below), keep longshore current in mind. Aim your cast a little up current so that when you retrieve, your lure sweeps straight in front of you when your retrieve is about halfway in.

Much has been written and said about the effects of winds and tides on striped bass fishing, but to tell the truth, I have never been able to find patterns that hold. Some extremely successful bass fishermen absolutely avoid dead low tide, others dislike any outgoing tide. Some surf fans will not fish when the water is dead calm. I would recommend ignoring any hard rules about tides and water conditions. Fish when you can, and use your head about where the fish might be and how to approach them.

Surf, Tackle, Lures and Bait

I hesitate to get too detailed with instructions about what kind of gear and tackle you will want or need for surf-fishing. If you are already in the game, you have equipment and I would only suggest that you try to keep it simple. If you are just getting started, however, here are a few tips.

Rods

The purpose of a surf rod is to be able to cast as easily as possible and for distance. My recommendation is to get one medium-sized spinning rod—try a fibreglass rod, about nine feet long, heavy enough to cast up to three ounces of weight—and a matching reel, capable of holding about 200 yards of 15-pound test monofilament line. Ask the dealer or bait store owner for some advice on this. You are after a medium-weight reel, one which will match your rod. Reels come in all colors, styles, and prices, some with enough gadgets to compute Greenwich Mean Time. Start with a simple, no-nonsense reel with as few adjustments and extras as you can find, but buy a well-known brand—Penn and Daiwa are two—and make sure it is for salt water (freshwater reels can rust and seize up overnight in salt water).

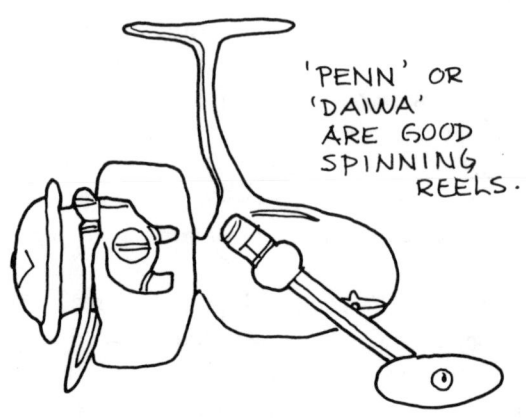

With such a rod and reel, you will be able to fish most of the northeast coast, using light and medium-weight lures. To check this out, you may want to visit a few local beaches and see what kinds of gear are being used. Ask fishermen. If they are not tied into a fish or grimly pursuing one, they will stop to chat. For starters, stay clear of big heavy surf sticks, up to twelve feet long with enormous butts, and stay clear of ultra-light tackle. Stay in the middle until you master the surf and until you decide you are in the battle for the duration. Then later, in special situations, you can add to your first equipment.

I recommend that you buy good monofilament line, 15-pound test, and that you change it once a year. You will be doing lots of casting and line does wear. It's cheaper to buy new line than to replace lures or rigging you snap off. To get extra use out of line, break off five or so feet every other time you go fishing to get rid of the worn end section, and halfway through the first season reverse the line to give the part near the spool some work. I also make it a point to keep my reel full. A filled spool casts farther and easier.

Wash your reel with fresh water when you can and keep it oiled. A good reel that is well cared for will last a decade or two.

Lures

Different parts of the coast have different "hot" lures, and they vary from season to season and year to year. You will probably see someone on the beach with a special tackle bag containing up to twenty lures, different kinds, colors, and sizes. Next to him will be someone with a lure tied on and one more in a shirt pocket. Some fishermen change lures every few casts. Others use one lure for two weeks. Your best bet is to go to the beach and see what successful fishermen are using and use that too. Or deck yourself out with four basic lures and then add or subtract as you gain experience. I almost always carry the following when I am after stripers in the surf with lures:

One Hopkins spoon, a hammered stainless steel, two ounces.
One Gibbs or Atom surface popper, blue and white, two ounces.
One Rebel, Rapala, or Redfin swimming plug, silver below, and black or blue above, five inches long.
One bucktail jig, two ounces, red, white, or yellow.

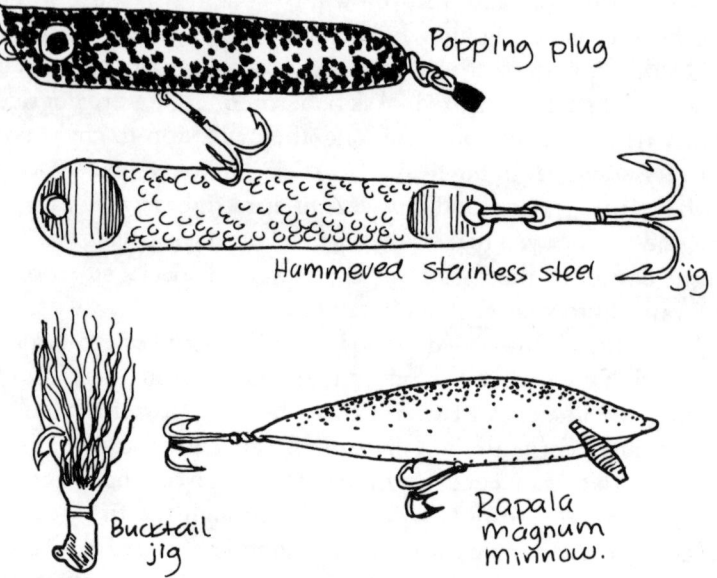

With these four lures, you can cover the surf from surface to bottom and imitate most of the bait that striped bass are interested in eating.

To attach these lures to your line and to be able to switch from one to the other, put a swivel clip on the end of your line, using an improved cinch knot. (And, by the way, that knot is the only knot you really need to know to tie monofilament.)

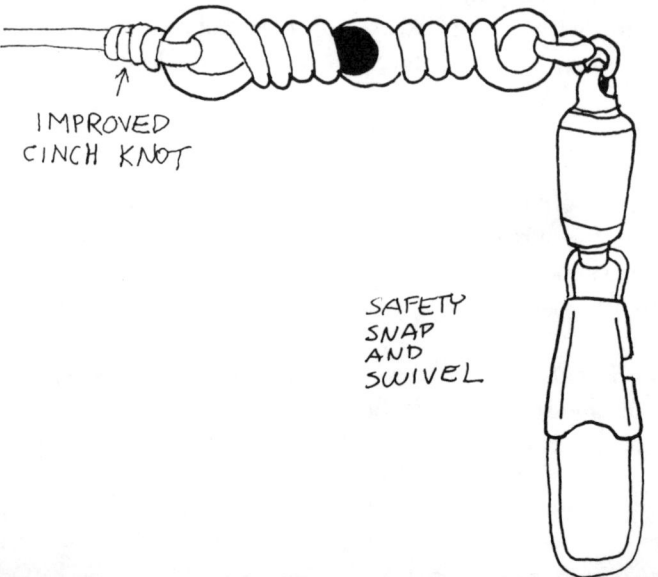

How to Fish the Lures

The spoon: This is the easiest of these lures to cast and work. It casts like a bullet. Zoom! You will think you are a champion when you give it a flip. Your retrieve can vary in speed. The faster you reel in, the closer the lure is to the surface. If you are casting on stripers that are breaking the surface, simply cast and reel immediately. If that doesn't produce fish, hesitate for a count of say five, and cut your retrieve speed in half. Or you can let the spoon drop to the bottom and retrieve in jerks to imitate a shrimp or sand lance.

Bass hitting a spoon will hook themselves. First sign of a fish is a sudden heavy weight on the line, followed by a slam-bang action. You need not strike your bass if it hooks itself. However, if you are getting hits and missing fish, try two techniques: either stop reeling for a second and let the fish catch up to the lure and hit again, or try striking firmly at the first indication of a hit.

Surface poppers: These take a little more skill. In the first place, they do not cast as well as spoons, especially in a head wind. Cast low into a strong wind, cast high into a following wind (this is true of all casting). A surface lure floats on the surface by itself. You provide the action by the speed of your retrieve and by jerking, wagging, or gently moving the rod

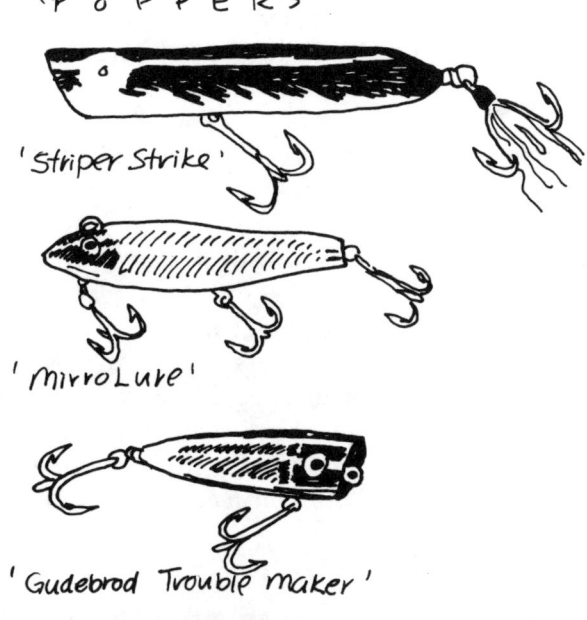

'POPPERS'

'Striper Strike'

'MirroLure'

'Gudebrod Trouble maker'

tip. Sometimes, a very rapid retrieve with sharp rod jerks, moving the lure six feet in a skitter, will get a strike. Other times, a slow retrieve with the plug gently flopping on the surface will do the trick. Most fishermen err on the side of retrieving too fast. Calm your urge and try slow speed.

Raising a striped bass on a surface lure is one of the great thrills of surf fishing, but don't be disappointed or surprised if you miss a few fish. I have missed more striped bass on surface poppers than with any other lure, but the sight of the fish rising and hitting more than makes up for the loss. If a bass swipes at your surface lure, but isn't hooked, stop your retrieve immediately. Let the lure sit there on the surface for five seconds or so. Give it a twitch, let it sit, then another twitch. Often this will entice the fish to give your plug another try. If that fails, fish the rest of the cast and then cast to the same place and draw the plug back through. Chances are very good that the fish will rise and hit again.

Here's an illustration. I was watching a very good fisherman on a beach one late summer afternoon. Mullet were running and he was casting a thin popping plug across deep water and onto the top of the bar. The tide was half in. In a period of one hour, he caught three bass, all around thirty pounds, and all were caught on second casts after they (or their twins) had swirled around the lure but missed it. Once, one bass made three swipes at the lure, great swirls of water, before it was hooked. All those bass appeared to be in a narrow band of water about sixty yards from shore. If the fisherman cast farther, no hits, and no hits inshore. The bass must have schooled on top of the bar snatching at passing mullet, and were enticed by surface lures retrieved in such a way that they looked enough like mullet to fool them.

Swimming plugs: These usually float until they are retrieved. They have a plastic lip that digs into the water and pulls the lure under when retrieved. The faster you retrieve them, the deeper they run. Again, most beginners reel too fast. A slow retrieve gives the plug a nice undulating action. Try different speeds, however, and don't be afraid to fish this lure carefully right in to shore. A forty-yard cast and a careful reel-in can sometimes deliver nothing until the last ten feet. Then a bass might hit the lure right in the wash.

Jigs: These should be fished on the bottom. Most jigs, often called bucktails, are for bottom fishing from boats, but as long as they weigh more than half an ounce and aren't loaded with feathers they cast well and should be part of your surf-fishing weaponry.

A jig is cast out, permitted to sink to the bottom and then jigged in or bounced on the bottom as it is retrieved. I find the best approach is to cast, wait a few seconds, take up the slack, and then jerk the tip of your rod up sharply about a foot. The jig will jump off the bottom a few inches and come in a foot or so. Then reel in the slack and repeat.

Jigging in the surf takes patience, especially if you have been casting other lures, because it takes quite a bit more time to retrieve a jig. I suppose jigs are imitating shrimp, crabs, or sand-burrowing fish. Though I have caught bass on jigs when all else failed, I have also cast jigs into visibly feeding bass schools without a touch. However, there are times when bass hug the bottom and only jigs will do the trick, so be sure to tuck one in your pocket for that once-in-a-hundred time when it will save you from a shutout.

JIGS

Hopkins Shorty Bucktail

Hopkins No-equal Bucktail

Bridgeport Feather Keel

Other lures: Remember, the basic four above are for starters. Use them as you begin to surf fish, but watch other fishermen and add to this basic list as you see it. Here are a few suggestions:

Plastic eels: These are life-like imitations of the real thing. They come in sizes from a few inches up to a foot and a half. I favor ten-inchers. They also come rigged with lead heads and usually a pair of hooks: they are ready to use.

Eels should be fished slowly on the bottom. An eel moves along the bottom like a snake. One way to perfect your retrieve is to cast the eel in water you can see down into (a swimming pool is super if you have an understanding neighbor). Cast the eel, let it sink, and then practice retrieval speed until your eel looks like an eel.

I like to fish eels alongside jetty rocks, especially at night. Be patient, cover all the spots, and go easy on the retrieve.

Eels

Single hook rig

Tandem Rig

Droppers: These are hooks with bucktail or feathers tied on. They should be secured on separate leaders either up a few feet from your lure or behind it. These droppers imitate small baitfish and often your big lure will attract the bass, but the dropper will hook it.

Some bass fishermen use a dropper routinely, just to be sure they always have one around when it is the only thing that will catch bass. And there will come a time when you will be casting in among bass, often big ones, who insist on eating only little two-inch anchovies or silversides. You can almost beat the bass over the head with a big lure and not catch them. That's the time for a dropper.

"Hot Lures": I was fishing one choppy fall day, doing nothing. A friend came up the beach and asked if I had a black and silver Rebel swimming plug. I did have one and I gave it to him. He clipped it on, went fifty yards down the beach and promptly landed a bass. I stayed with a yellow and white Redfin and caught nothing. That day (or week), black and silver Rebels were hot.

All veteran bass fishermen have run into hot lure situations, times when one special design does the work. Often, a new lure will seem to catch bass consistently the first year or so it is on the market. Some lures, the Florida Shiner is an example, seem to make comebacks, hot for a year, cold for ten, then back in the hot seat.

My recommendation here is to go to the hot lure, if it is catching fish, and your lure is not. This means watching fishermen and their catch and adapting your tactics accordingly.

Finders Keepers: If you find a lure on the beach, give it a try. Why not? It's free. It might have been tossed by a fish recently. Anyway, it's a gift, so accept it gratefully and get it wet.

Lure Confidence: Fish each lure as if it is just ready to be attacked by a fish. Most successful fishermen *know* the lure they are using will catch fish, so they work and concentrate, and that effort pays off.

Bait

Bait-fishing is a sit-and-wait game and most baits are fished right on or close to the bottom (except for some live baits covered later). However, the rules for "reading" the surf still hold. You will need to know something about the water out there, how deep it is and what the current is doing, because you are trying to figure out where the fish are so you can get your bait to them.

The rig: The bait rig is often called terminal tackle, for it rests on the opposite end from the fisherman. The simplest rig is a weight (sinker, dipsey) and a hook-on-leader. Here is a standard rig for striped bass:

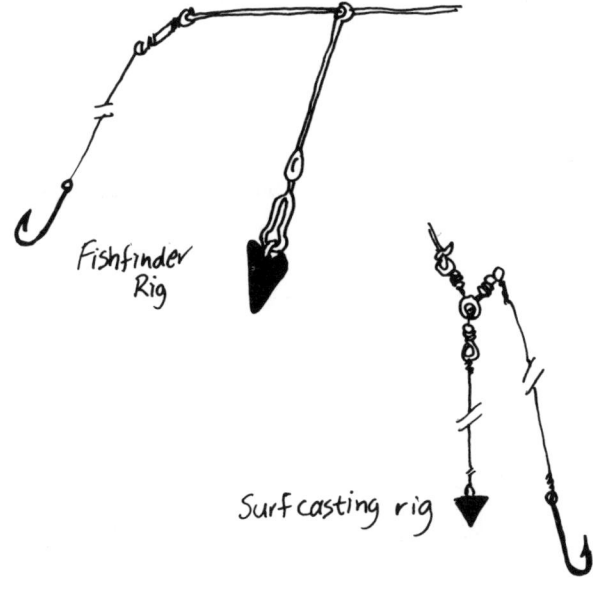

Bass have big, tough mouths, so your hooks should be big. I favor a 4/0 size—that's about as big as a dime. Hooks should have little reverse barbs on the shank to hold the bait stretched out, especially worms. To avoid twisting and kicking, use a three-way swivel. One eye of the swivel takes your line, the second your weight (attached with a clip), the third your hook.

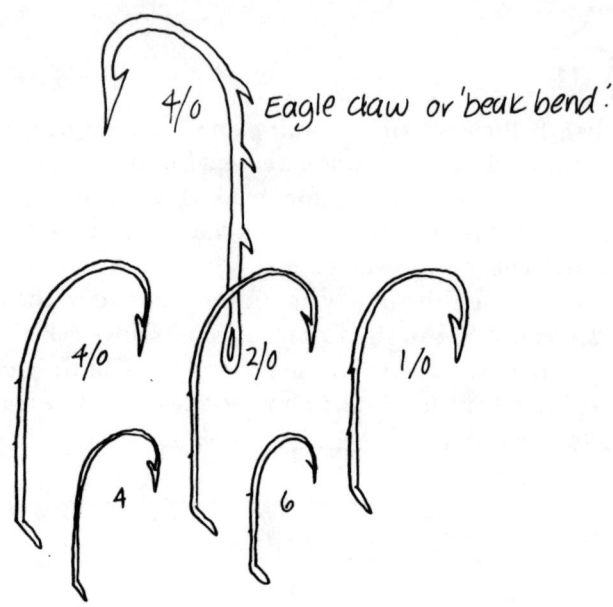

Your weight should be heavy enough to cast and to hold bottom but not too heavy for your rod. I try to use the lightest weight possible to do the job, usually around two ounces, and I use pyramids for sand bottoms because they hold better, and rounded weights on rough bottoms because they are less likely to snag.

WEIGHTS

Pyramid: Best for sand bottoms.

Rounded: best for rough bottoms.

The leader should be strong stuff. I use 40-pound test monofilament. Remember, the leaders get rough treatment on the bottom especially if it rubs (you hope) against the heads of a few hooked bass.

Some fishermen favor a "fish finder" rig. This allows the line to pass through a ring on the sinker, so the bait is essentially tied straight to the line. The theory is that the bait can drift around covering more ground and that a wary fish, picking up the bait, will not feel the drag of the weight. I am not convinced that a "fish finder" is any better than the standard rig.

Sometimes it pays to have your bait slightly off the bottom. To do this, buy leadered (snelled) hooks with thin cork floats attached, or you can rig your own. When crabs are especially hungry, it pays to have your bait up off the bottom a few inches, particularly if you are using worms at 25¢ a throw.

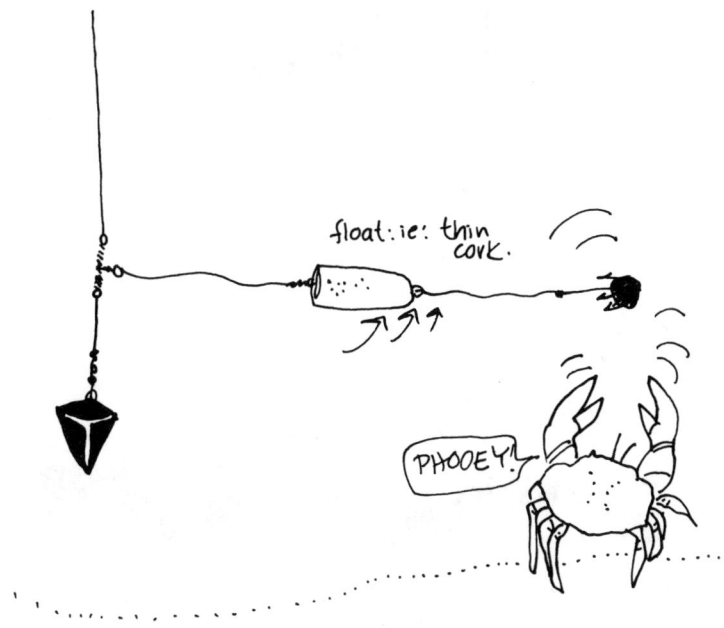

The baits: The three most commonly used surf baits for striped bass are worms, crabs, and clams. They are relatively interchangeable, depending on your pocketbook and their availability.

Worms are probably the universal first choice, because they are a natural bait, a natural striped bass food. They are also easy to rig and cast.

Sand worms are the favorite, bought at bait stores or dug in marshes. They can be twelve inches long and as big around as a pencil. They should be rigged so they fish stretched out—this makes clear the value of the bait hook described above. Try to avoid a ball of worm meat. In nature, worms are extended. Try to duplicate that mode. Remember, too, that marine worms are nocturnal. They spend their days dug into the bottom and their nights feeding. Worms are therefore good night bait.

Calico or lady crabs (the ones that bite your toes when you swim in the surf) are useful striper baits. Best are softshells, crabs that have just shed their hard shell. They can be found in surf sloughs at low tide, using a crab rake. Softshells need to be tied on the hook. Or you can use hard crabs. Take off the top shell and the legs and claws. Big crabs should be cut in half. Crabs should be fished right on the bottom.

Clams: The biggest striper I ever caught fell to a clam bait, although it was partly accidental because I was going after black drum in the surf at the time. You can use surf clams or hard clams. Cut away the really soft part of the clam, and use the tougher foot or tongue. Some fishermen swear by clams after a storm, which they say will have churned up the bottom and dug out and cracked up some clams that were in the sand near the surf's edge. I haven't been able to prove this one either way, but clams do work, though I would put them third after worms and crabs.

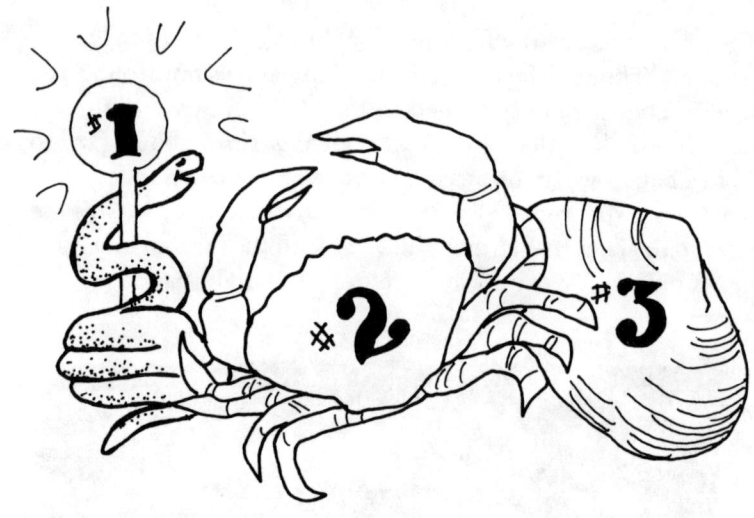

Fish chunks will sometimes snare bass, either half of big bunker, spot, or mackerel, or whole smaller fish. They are not high on my list, however.

In general, with bait as with lures, it pays to check with bait dealers and fishermen and follow the leaders.

The list of foods found in striper's stomach is almost endless and it is always possible to catch them with such things as squid, sand fleas, green crabs, blood worm pieces, and shrimp, so don't rule out *any* bait.

Live bait: **Probably more large (you could even say huge) striped bass are caught on live bait than any other way, and menhaden lead the list of live baits. Menhaden or bunker, or pogy in New England, are large herrings. They reach two pounds and can be fished live at any size though fishermen favor fish under a pound for casting ease, if nothing else.**

The easy way to fish live bunker is to find a school of bunker close enough to cast over. Use a bare treble hook or a Hopkins if that's all you have. Then, when you have foul-hooked a bunker, stop reeling and let the bunker swim around with your hook in it and hope that a big bass decides to take its meal. You can bring the bunker in to make sure it is hooked well—it should be hooked gently in the back—but it is easier just to leave the fish and your hook out there, saving a cast.

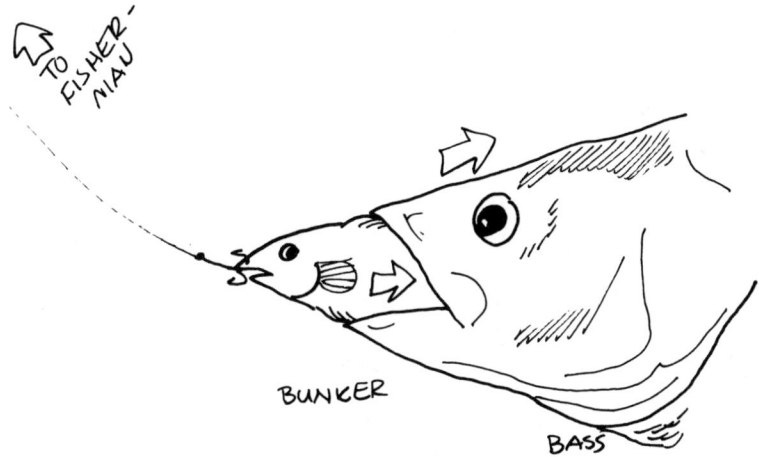

A hooked bunker seems to have great attraction for bass. It swims differently, usually dropping back from the school and below it. It will also swim irregularly. Predator fish, of which the striper is a prime example, appear to find this enticing, and they will single out your bunker for attack.

If there are no bunker schools around, you will need to bring your own bunker with you. This means keeping them alive in a bucket of water by using a battery operated aerator. You can fish bunker dead, giving them some life by working your rod, but live bunker far outfish dead ones.

A special note about fishing live bunker. Stripers feed by swallowing their prey whole, and they favor the head first method for fish so the spines don't stick in their throats. The bass that grabs your live bunker will try to swivel the fish around in its mouth until it's heading throatward before swallowing. This means that you must not be tempted to strike hard when you first feel a hit. Give the striper time to mouth the bunker, get it lined up, and, if you can stand the tension, swallow it. If you strike too soon, you will pull the bunker out of the striper's mouth. One way to tell if you have done this is to retrieve your bunker and look at it. If it shows some pinch marks and is missing lots of scales, chances are you pulled your bait out of a striper's mouth. If the bait comes in cut cleanly in two, that's a bluefish hit.

Although this kind of fishing is not my favorite, there is a part of it that I find very exciting. Say you have hooked your bunker well and cast it as gently as possible into the surf. Then, as the bunker swims, you give it line and you walk parallel to the beach as it moves. Usually the bunker will be under water a foot or so, and some will head toward the bottom. Then you will see your bunker move to the surface, break water, and swim in panic: below it lurks the bass of your dreams. Be cool, let the bunker do what it wants and maybe you will be rewarded with the swirl, the inhalation, the thud, the move, and the felt weight of a monster coming up for its big meal.

Other fish can be used the same way: mackerel, mullet, spot, and small bluefish, but bunker seem to have it all: size, attraction, and ability to live through the strain.

We spoke of plastic eels above. Some fishermen use live eels, especially at night near rocks, but eels have a way of swimming right into holes and taking themselves out of the game. So, use dead eels, rigged and fished to appear alive. Here are some drawings to show you how to rig eels.

Get eels about ten inches long, and you can re-use them by chucking them into the freezer. Or they can be salted.

1. Provide eels, long needle, head jigs, scissors, 7/0 hook snelled with a piece of doubled 80-pound Dacron line

2. Run needle through body from behind the vent to the mouth. Hook ends of tail hook line into eye of needle.

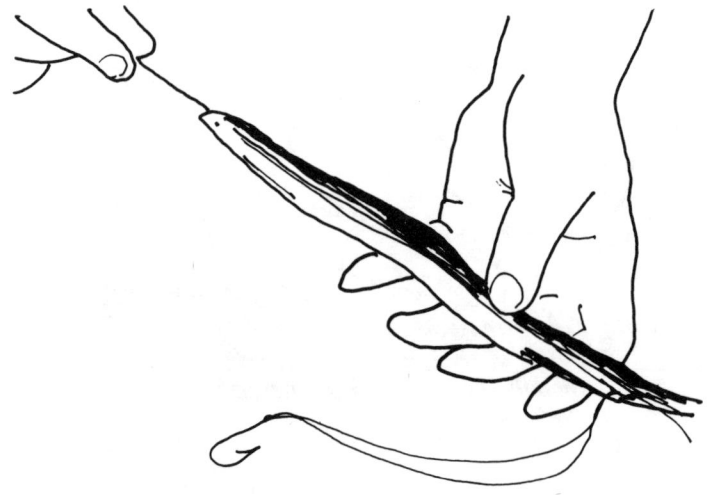

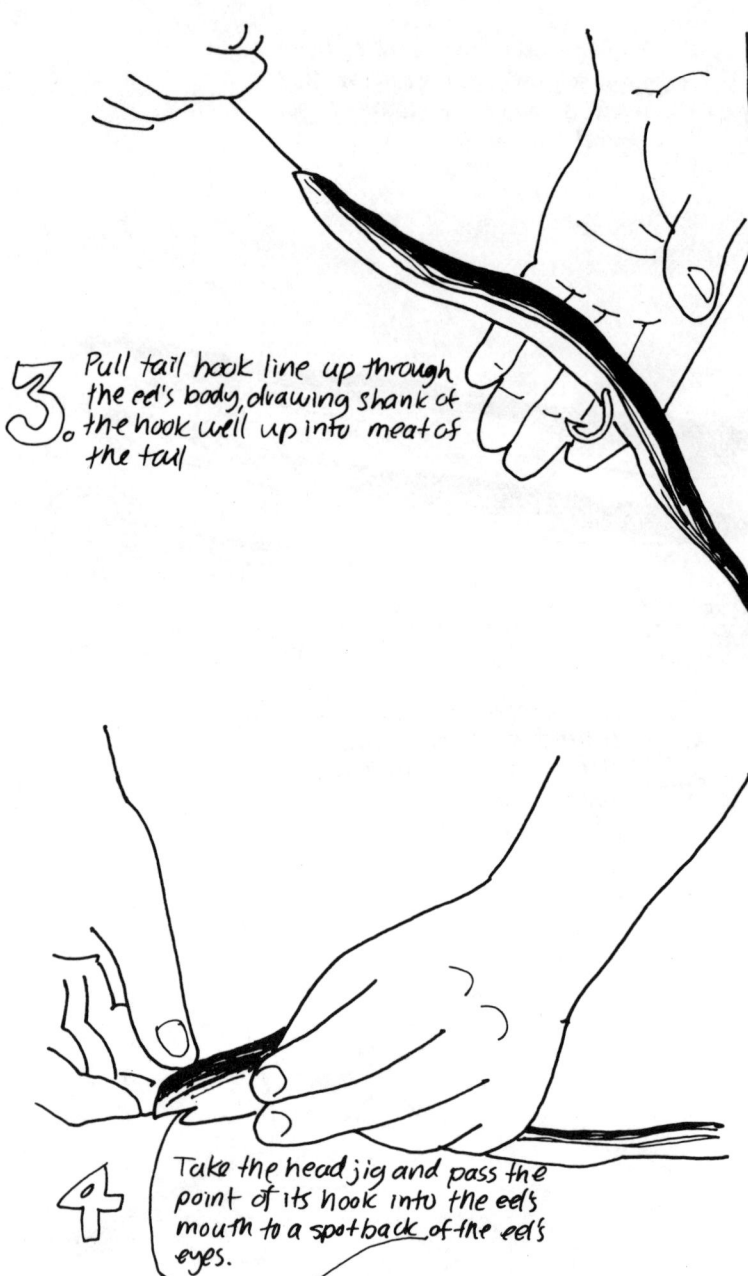

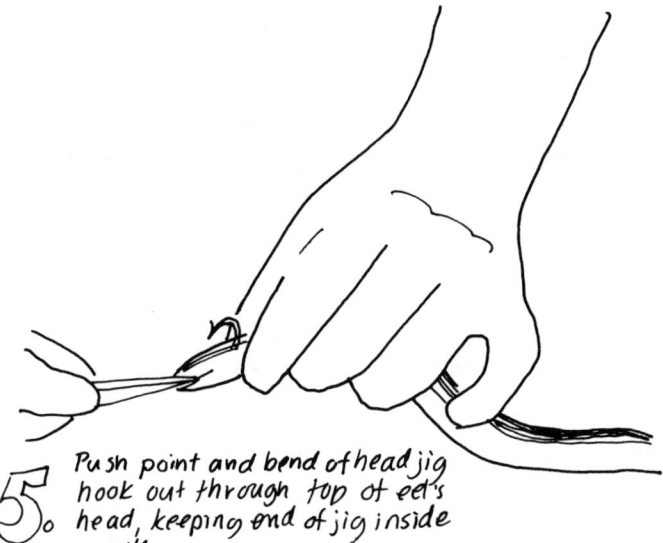

5. Push point and bend of head jig hook out through top of eel's head, keeping end of jig inside mouth.

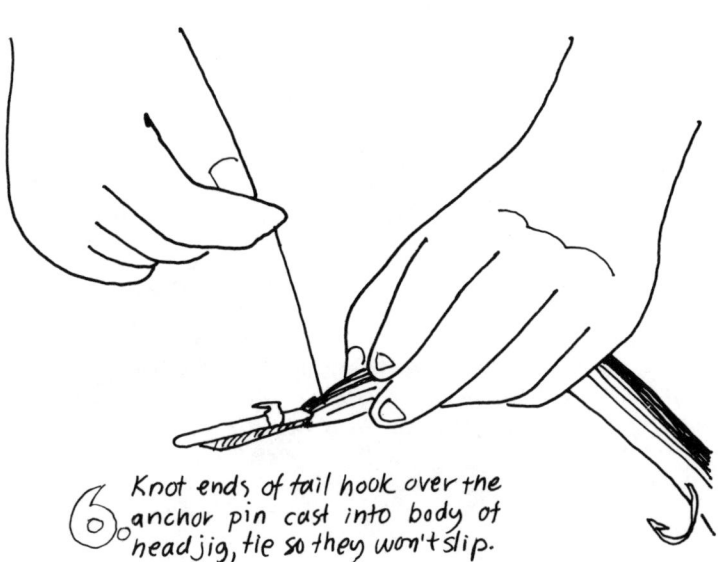

6. Knot ends of tail hook over the anchor pin cast into body of head jig, tie so they won't slip.

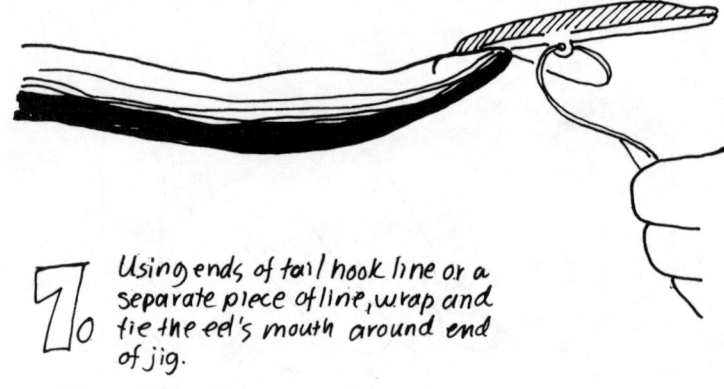

7. Using ends of tail hook line or a separate piece of line, wrap and tie the eel's mouth around end of jig.

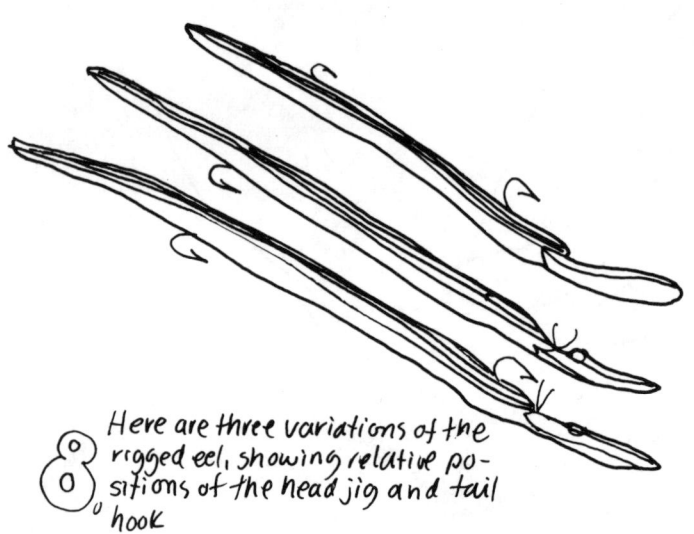

8. Here are three variations of the rigged eel, showing relative positions of the head jig and tail hook

As for *where* to cast all this bait, tactics are not much different from those with lures except that you will most often be blind fishing, that is casting and fishing where you think stripers might be, rather than looking for signs of fish swirling. This is a good time to point out that if you are bait fishing, you should have a lure or two tucked away in case fish start to show. If that happens, abandon your bait and go with lures.

Otherwise, look for beach irregularities, holes, bars, cuts in bars, jetties, sloughs, and, if you don't have any luck, move and try again. Above all with bait fishing, be alert, because the largest of striped bass can nudge the bait lightly. Don't let the size of the bite fool you.

In surf summary

Travel light, look for signs—choppy water, birds, swirls—change tactics if you're doing nothing, watch other fishermen and be ready to copy their success.

3. OTHER SHORE FISHING

I have used the term surf fishing to mean standing right on the beach and in the waves, but there are other kinds of fishing from shore. Many of the practices are similar, but there are a few tricks peculiar to each kind of fishing. Here are a few of them, keeping in mind general surf fishing logic:

Jetty Fishing

Properly, a jetty is a rock structure at an inlet and a groin is a similar structure on a plain beachfront, but I'll call all such rocks "jetties" primarily because that's what most fishermen call them and they, in turn, are called "jetty jockeys" by outdoor writers.

You can fish a jetty by standing on the beach at its base and casting out, thus fishing the water close to the rocks, or you can climb out on the jetty and fish its end and the sides. The end of a jetty is prime striped bass habitat, because there are usually jumbled rocks there that have been ripped off the jetty by storm waves. The sides of the jetty, too, will have rocks below the waterline. Fish these rock edges and submerged rocks thoroughly with swimmers, metal, and eels—the latter especially at night—and fish your lure right up to the last turn of the reel, because bass are often right up against the rocks.

Pay special attention to the times of tides when fishing jetties, and also fish different jetties. As you get to know them well, you will find favorite spots, and favorite times and tides. In general, tides flooding in the late evening and the early morning are my favorite times. When the wind is blowing strongly down the beach, jetties often provide a good lee for fishing. Be sure, however, to try fishing both sides; striped bass will often be in the strong surge on the windy side, especially if bait is trapped there.

Bank Fishing

Striper fishing along the edges of estuaries, bays, and rivers is productive in spring and fall when bass are moving either downriver toward the sea for coastal migrations and feeding or upriver toward their wintering grounds. In fact, the earliest spring bass are almost always taken in tidal rivers—the Mullica, the Hudson, the Connecticut. They are usually caught with worms in late March, as water temperatures reach into the forties. The best places to fish are on the edges of sod banks with steep drops, especially where a stream enters or the water cuts into the bank forming eddies.

Or you can wade the hard bottoms along the edges of rivers, casting lures out toward channel edges, letting the lure drift across the current and retrieving it with short jerks.

Another method is to drift worms, but this is covered under the next section on boat fishing.

Often, fall stripers are schoolies, short fish up to fourteen inches and you should go for them with small lures; bucktails are good and so are small spoons and swimmers. Often fishing for schoolies is fast and furious in November, as the fish feel the urge for one last big feed before wintertime slow down.

Bridge Fishing

Any low bridge or causeway across salt or brackish water is worth watching for striper action. If you drive across a bridge and notice, especially at night, that a few people are fishing over the bridge, check it out. They may be going for and getting stripers. This is common in the Chesapeake Bay area, where many of the bridges cross parts of the bay and its tributaries. It is prime fishing right into winter if the weather holds. Bucktails bounced on the bottom are the number one method.

4. FISHING FOR STRIPERS FROM BOATS

You can catch a striped bass from any kind of boat. I have taken bass from a sixteen-foot canoe in a tidal river and I am sure you could even troll up Chesapeake Bay on an oil tanker if you could slow the ship down enough. But the beauty of boat fishing for stripers is that they are seldom far from shore, so you can go out for them in *small* boats. Just keep an eye on the weather and run for cover if things get nasty.

A lot of nice striped bass are caught off Long Island and New Jersey in the fall by cartoppers, who carry twelve to sixteen foot aluminum boats around on the roofs of their cars and launch from the surf. The standard Cuttyhunk bass boat is seldom more than twenty-five feet long; likewise, boats that fish the famed Montauk Point area. And the protected Chesapeake can be covered with small boats also.

Much of what you learn about striped bass in the surf can be applied to fishing for bass from boats. The lures are similar and you should be looking for the same type of water—places where tides or currents meet to cause churning water, irregularities of bottom, reefs reaching toward the surface or deep holes in otherwise shoal areas. Medium-weight surf rods also make good boat rods, although there are a few other types of rods and equipment you will also need.

The Boat

If you have a boat that floats you can use it for striped bass fishing. You can use your inboard, your outboard, your cabin cruiser, or your sailboat.

If you have no boat and you want to jump into the striped bass game, look hard before you leap. It is easy to spend more money than you anticipated; a bass boat can cost as much as three or four cars. Your best bet, if the bass boat bug bites, is to make friends with a serious boat fisherman and go out on a few trips with him. Or charter a small boat from any one of dozens of ports from Gloucester to Norfolk. Check out their gear and tactics and see if you won't be satisfied with a few trips a year on someone else's boat, instead of your own.

But let's say that you have a boat, either a brand new guaranteed bass killer or the old clunker with a few more years left in it. Here is a rundown of the equipment you will want, at least at the start, and then some suggestions about tactics. I will leave out any talk of specific boat equipment, things like engines, fuels, compass, cushions. This is boat business and you either know about it or you don't.

Consider the following equipment:

Trolling: A six-foot medium action rod is the best all-purpose rod for striper trolling. It should carry a 3/0 to 4/0 reel with a forty-pound test monofilament or dacron line.

Casting: A medium- or light-weight surf rod (or one a little shorter) will do the trick, with reel and line to match.

Jigging: The surf rod mentioned above will do in a pinch, but any seven- to eight-foot medium action rod will do, with either spinning or conventional reel, with twenty- to thirty-pound test.

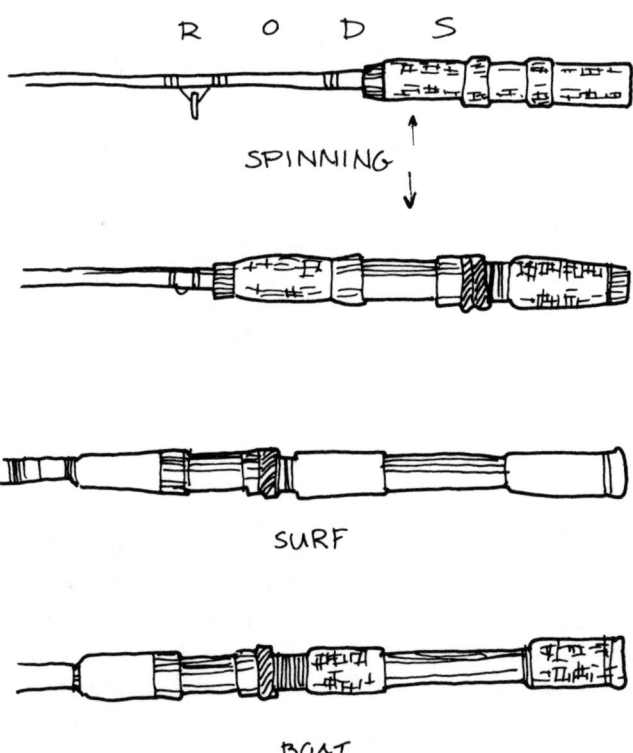

RODS

SPINNING

SURF

BOAT

Other: I usually take along a light spinning rod and reel too, with ten-pound test in case a school of smaller fish shows on the surface and I want to get at them with small lures. But light tackle should be used with care if there are three or four fishermen on the boat because you can tangle a lot of lines and lose a lot of friends fighting a larger fish all around the boat, while your fishing mates must either dodge your line or pull out and wait for you to finish.

Lures, Baits: Many of the lures and baits described in the section on surf fishing are usable from boats, the only real difference being the addition of a few trolling lures. Start with some of those listed above, especially the swimming plugs. However, bigger plugs can be trolled, and there are a few special to trolling.

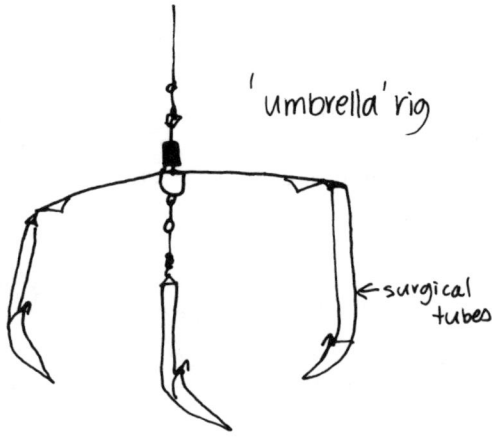

One of the favorites is the *Tube Lure*. These are surgical tubes rigged with hooks to imitate eels or fish. They can be as small around as a thin pencil and a few inches long, up to as big as a small banana. Rigged in series and combination, they become an umbrella or gorilla rig, a fearsome set of up to twelve lures on a wire frame, the whole device trolled to look like a small school of bait fish.

Other Equipment: For trolling, different types of weighted lines or trolling weights will be needed. They are covered under trolling. A landing net for small fish and a gaff for larger fish is important because you will not be able to retrieve the fish up the beach on waves, as you do when surf fishing, but will have to yank it from the water into the boat.

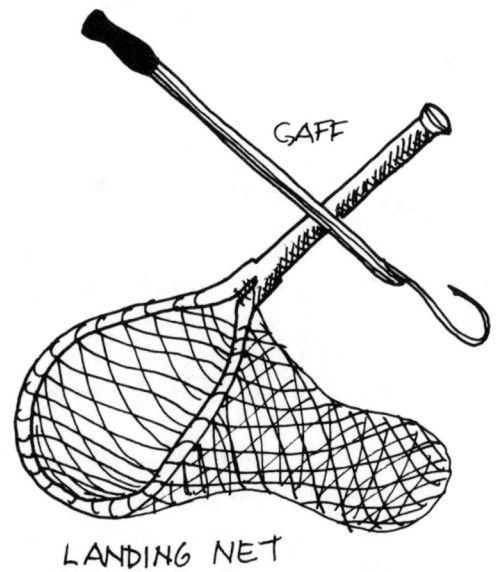

Fathometers, Sounders: These are valuable tools for finding both the bottom and the fish, especially when you are trolling or jigging. They work by sending an energy pulse downward through the water and recording the echo or return on the energy from the bottom to the device. They also show anything between the boat and the bottom, meaning fish. There are two types of such devices, those that record tracings on paper and those that indicate by flashes of light on a screen. The latter are usually cheaper, but you will need to keep an eye on them to get the readings. The tracers record permanently on paper so you can see the record of what happened below as your boat passed over. Here are some examples of each:

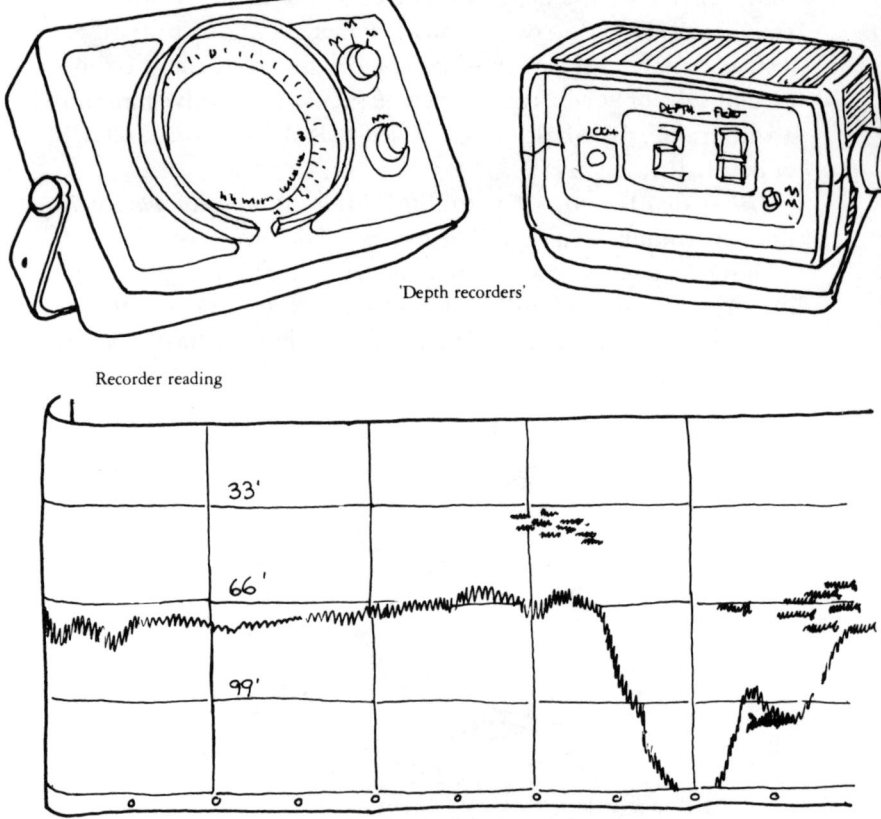

'Depth recorders'

Recorder reading

There are two basic methods for fishing for striped bass from boats. One is trolling, the other casting, including jigging.

Trolling for Striped Bass

Trolling is an especially useful way to fish for bass if there are no signs of fish, no breaking schools or bird activity, and no good recent reports of where the fish might be hanging out. By trolling, you can cover a lot of water searching for fish. Then when you do find them, you can mark the spot by taking a few bearings or dropping over a marker, either a simple float or a float attached to line and a weight. Then you can come back and troll through the same area.

However, all trolling should be done with a plan. Here are a few techniques that have worked for me:

—Go where the other boats are. If other good bass fishermen are working an area, work the area yourself. It's no sin to benefit from someone else's expertise, as long as you don't crowd other boats.

—Fish the rips. Head for any area where the water surface shows an irregularity, a place where the tide-driven water butts into unmoving water, or where water wells up or pushes across a reef or bar. You can fish these rips up and down and across the tide, trying all speeds and directions until something happens.

—Fish edges. If you know a channel cut, fish the edge where the water starts its sudden drop down the sides of the channel.

—Fish in close to shore, covering the areas that you wish you could reach if you were surf casting. One such prime spot is the water just off the outer bar, which you can cover by trolling either with or against the current. Or find the cut in the bar (or enter from the ends) and fish the slough inside, taking care to keep an eye on the sea so you don't swamp or run around. See the drawings for some suggested trolling tactics along the beach.

—Troll up and down the beach, not from shore out. Almost all of my trolling success has been while on a run parallel to the beach, and I have not caught a bass more than two miles from shore.

—Keep your eyes open for surface action, and be ready to haul in the trolling gear and switch to surface plug casting if a school does break. By all means avoid running through a school of fish. Try to fish the edges so the school doesn't sound.

—Trolling depth is important:

—Watch your sounder and when you see marks of fish, adjust your trolling depth.

—Learn your boat's speed and rpms so you will know how deep your lures are at various speeds; when in doubt, troll slowly.

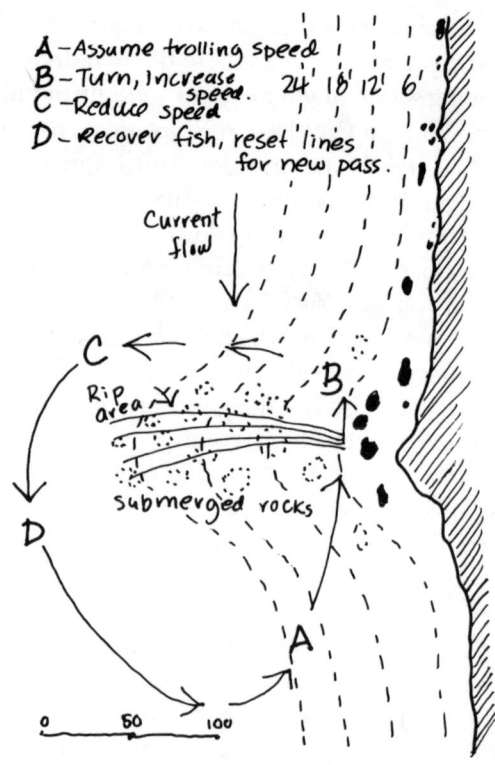

Trolling pattern for a rocky point. The boat swings inshore, against the current, with all lines out and ready at "A". At "B" the boat turns offshore to "C", increasing speed to a fast troll so lures will not hang up on the rocks. The boat slows to a very slow troll by the time it has crossed the 24 foot depth line, permitting lures to sink as the water deepens. Hooked fish are recovered at "D".

A — Assume trolling speed
B — Turn, increase speed
C — Reduce speed
D — Recover fish, reset lines for new pass.

Trolling pattern for an ocean bar. The boat enters the slough between bar and beach by passing through one of the deeper holes in the bar. Water inside the bar may be 15 to 20 feet deep, permitting the use of wire line tackle. Seas breaking on the bar usually spend their force before they become dangerous to the boat. Speed may be fast or slow, depending on the type of trolling lures selected.

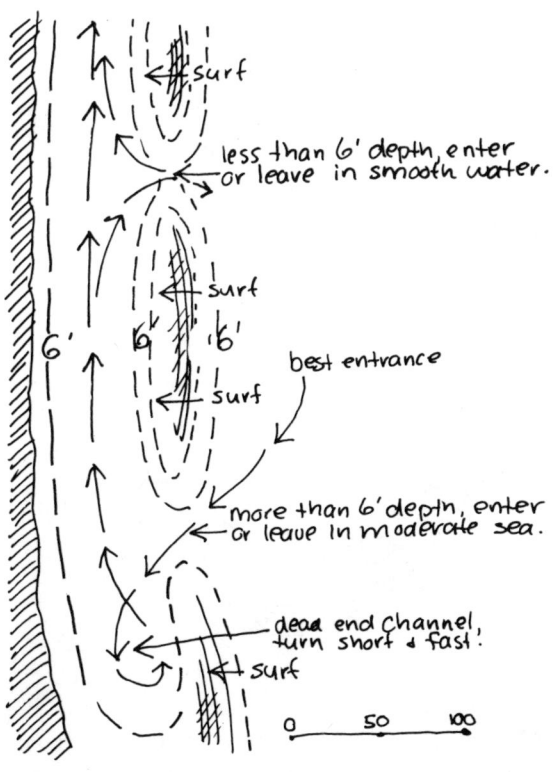

There are a number of ways to get your lure down. First, use wire line. This heavier line will drop your lure. Or use trolling weights, such as these:

Some trolling weights:

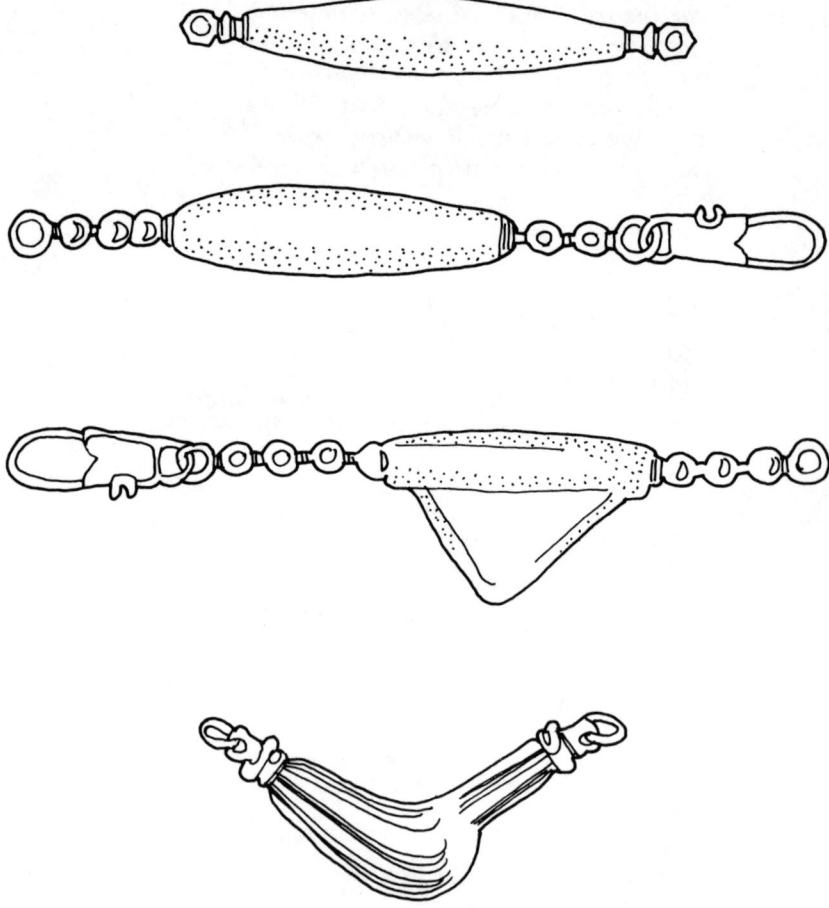

The slower you are moving and the more line you have out, the deeper your lure will be. Also, when you turn the boat, the lure drops toward the bottom, so either speed up and make the turn gradual, or bring in line so the lure doesn't grab bottom.

Casting and Jigging From Boats

I prefer this to trolling. You get a much better feel of the fish and it gets you doing something instead of sitting watching the tip of your trolling rod. Also, it's quieter and it saves fuel.

In this kind of fishing, you can think of the boat as a moveable platform to fish from and you can apply all the rules of surf fishing to your search. First of all, if fish are breaking and birds are screaming, the job of finding fish is easy. Remember to approach a feeding school quietly or the fish might spook. I try to figure which way the school is moving and get ahead of it and slightly off to one side, casting into the leading edge. You can also get up behind a school and cast into its rear guard. Sometimes when the breaking fish themselves aren't hitting, a jig under or behind the school will pick up fish.

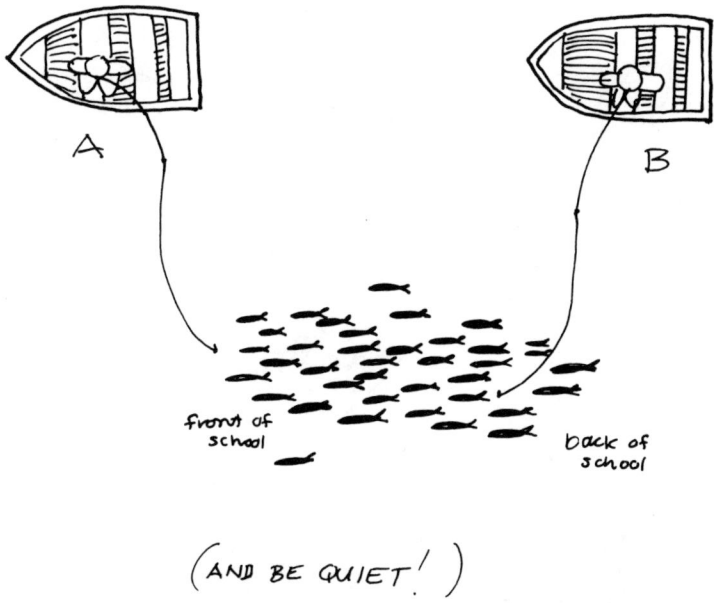

If the fish aren't showing, head into the beach or toward a reef or shoal area and fish the edges, the top, the up and down current ends. If the winds and currents are kind, you can drift along the outside of the outer bar, casting onto its edge and across the top, or you can get inside the bar and then cast out over it and in toward shore.

All jetties are worth a look, and from a boat, this is your chance to really cover the outer tip of the jetty, which usually has a jumble of rock underwater worth working.

If you have a livewell, you can bring along some bunker or mackerel and let them swim across the bars and around the jetties to attract bass.

One recommendation: don't crowd in on fishermen fishing from the beach or the jetty. If they were there first, give them a break. After all, you can cover a lot of water with your boat, while they are limited to the amount of water they can reach from shore. There is a practical side to this recommendation. There are surf fishermen who will fire a treble-hook across your bow to chase you off if they think you are too close. Better another spot to fish than a scalp full of hooks.

River Stripers by Boat
One of my favorite pastimes is to launch a small boat or canoe on a quiet river in a cool sunrise and go out casting or drifting for spring bass. I've caught nice bass in Indian River, the Mullica, the Navesink, the Hudson, the Connecticut, Narragansett Bay, and Pleasant Bay on Cape Cod, all with the same three basic tactics.

First, motor or paddle along the flats of the river, near the banks, casting small swimming or popping plugs. Look for bass in coves, at the channel edges, and on shallow grass or mud flats.

Second, drift the main river channel with a rig that carries a long fat seaworm a foot or so off the bottom.

Third, if you can't find fish with these tactics, try a slow troll up- or downriver, especially where a creek enters or the river enters a bay. Often you can find a school by trolling and can then cut the motor and cast into the fish.

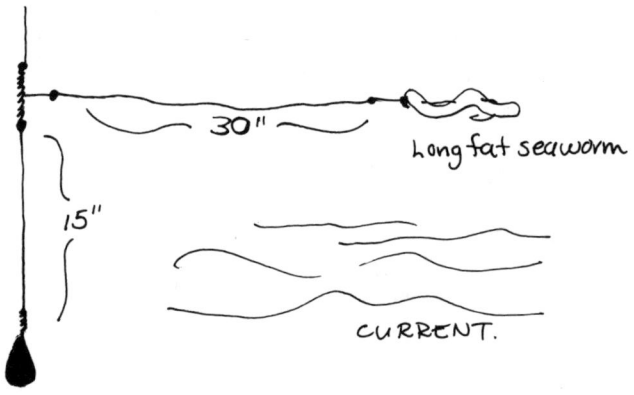

5. THE FUTURE OF THE STRIPED BASS

East coast bass populations swing up and down primarily in relation to the success of breeding in Chesapeake Bay, the term "breeding" to cover spawning and growth through the larval stage to about three to four inches. Biologists in the Bay have sampled fingerling populations of bass for decades, charting the successes or failures of year-classes. Their studies show a series of good year-classes up until about the middle of the 1970s and then a progression of less than good breeding years. This shows up in reduced landings of striped bass beginning in 1977. Best spawning years in the Bay were 1958, 1961, 1964, 1966, and 1970. The worst were 1957, 1959, and 1980.

Because striped bass are so important as both game and commercial species, they have been subject to broad studies and different regulations to protect their population. It is the only eastern coastal marine species subject to size and creel limits (besides the salmon and, in New York, the fluke). As a fisherman, you should be aware that these limits vary, state to state.

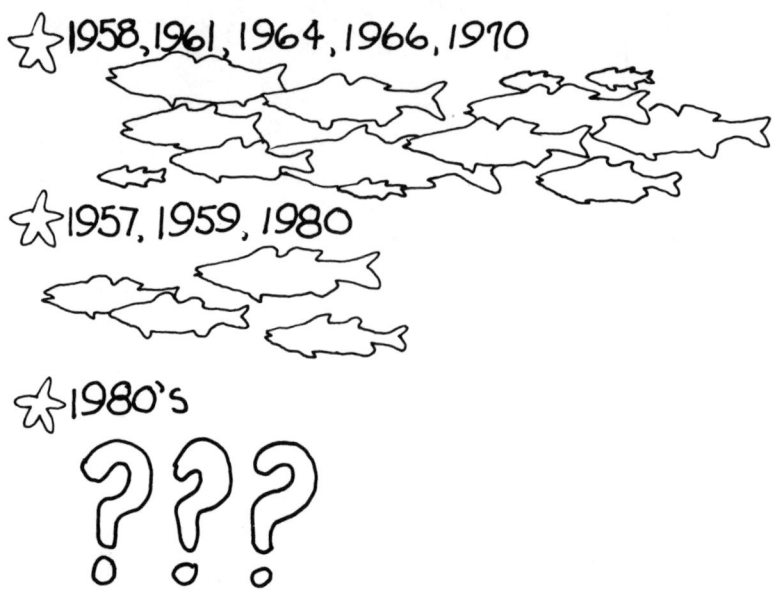

They can be tabulated as follows:

State	Minimum Size	Daily Creel Limit
New Hampshire	16"	none
Massachusetts	16"	none
Rhode Island	16"	none
Connecticut	16"	none
New York	16"	none
New Jersey	18"	10
Delaware	none	none
Maryland	12"	none
Virginia	14"	none
North Carolina	12"	none

These regulations are subject to change, however, because of the current shortages of striped bass, so it makes sense to check with other anglers before you start keeping too many too short bass.

Suffice it to say, you shouldn't take more bass than either the law or your stomach and freezer dictate. Don't be afraid to turn loose a big bass with a tag in it so you can have the thrill of finding out where your bass went and how fast it grew. And remember that if it is more than twenty-five pounds, it's a female and will spawn if freed.

6. CARING FOR, CLEANING AND COOKING YOUR CATCH

Striped bass make excellent eating. The flesh is firm and white. The care of a freshly-caught bass is no different from that of any other fish. Keep it as cool as possible, eat it soon after you catch it, or freeze it quickly in serving-size packets. If you can get your fish on ice do so. Otherwise, keep it out of the sun by covering it with a damp cloth, or, if you are on the beach, bury it in wet sand. Don't forget to mark the spot!

Bass may either be scaled or skinned. I prefer scaling fish if they are ten pounds or less, and if I plan to eat them right away, but I prefer to freeze skinned striper.

To scale, keep the fish damp so the scales are soft. Hold the fish by the head and run a scaler or the back of a knife against the grain of the scales, working from the tail toward the head. Rinse after scaling.

If you plan to skin the fish, there are two techniques: skin it before you dress it or after. Use a sharp, pointed knife with some flexibility so you can work the knife close to the bone. To skin a bass before dressing it, make a shallow cut down either side of the dorsal (top) fin from head to tail. Make the next cut from the top back behind the head down across the fish's belly and toward the vent (anus, rear end). Then continue to cut down to the tail. Free the skin from the flesh at the top of the head, grasp the skin with pliers, and pull. The skin should come off in one swoop. Now, go back and repeat the incisions, this time making them deeper and keeping the knife close to the bone, from dorsal to ventral, then back toward the tail. You will end up with two boneless fillets of bass, ready for pan or freezer.

Or, you can fillet the bass first and then skin it. Place the fillet skin side down and get your knife between the flesh and the skin at the tail. Then draw the knife toward the shoulder section, while moving the tail section back and forth in a sawing motion.

Another, possibly even better, way to clean a bass is to watch someone else do it and learn by copying. It is not the easiest process to describe, even with drawings, but cleaning a fish need not be made out to be a task for magicians. Just remember, you can eat everything on a fish except the head, the guts, and the bones, and even the head has some good meat on it and can be boiled up for fish stock or soup.

Striped bass freezes well. Freeze it in packets that you can eat in a sitting. A good trick is to put the bass in plastic bags or containers, or paper milk cartons and fill them with water before freezing. This surrounds the fish with water and keeps out air.

Filleting a striped bass: the first incision is made, just skin deep, along the back, from base of head to base of tail. The cut is made on each side of the dorsal spine.

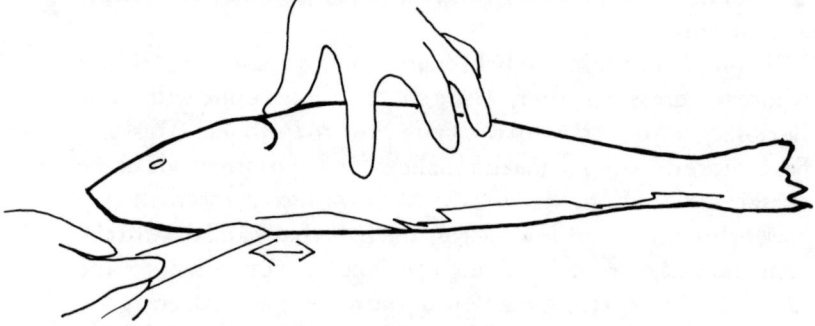

Then another incision is made over the side of the bass just behind the head, from the cut on the line to a spot just past the ventral fin.

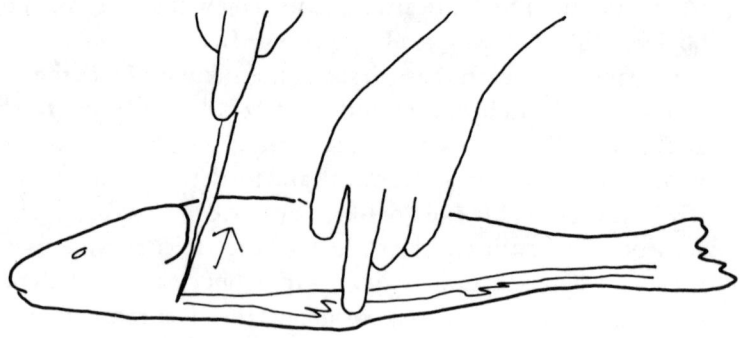

The incision is then followed along the bottom or belly of the fish, still just breaking the skin, all the way back to the base of the tail.

With a filleting knife, cut away the skin from the flesh in the area shown.

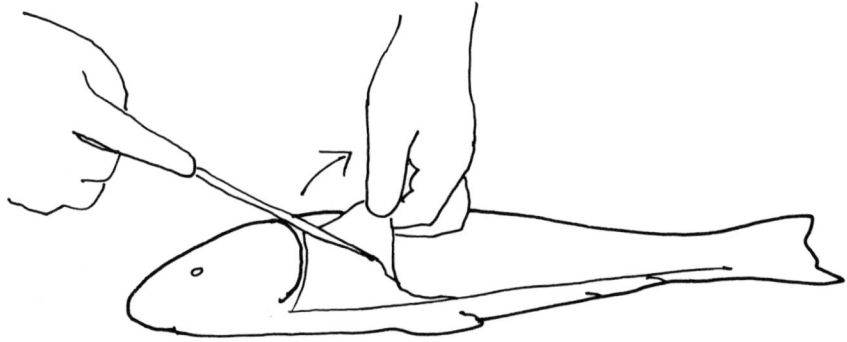

When you have freed enough skin from the flesh to grasp it with your pliers, hold the head and flesh down with one hand and quickly pull the skin off the flesh with the other. Pull it all the way to the base of the tail.

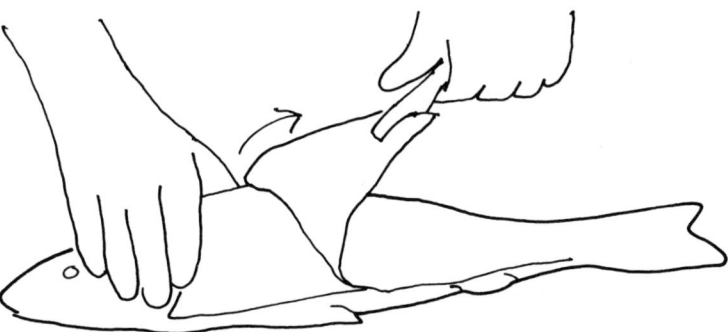

With the filleting knife, deepen the incision on the back, following the long spines in to the backbone. Free the fillet from head to tail along the backbone.

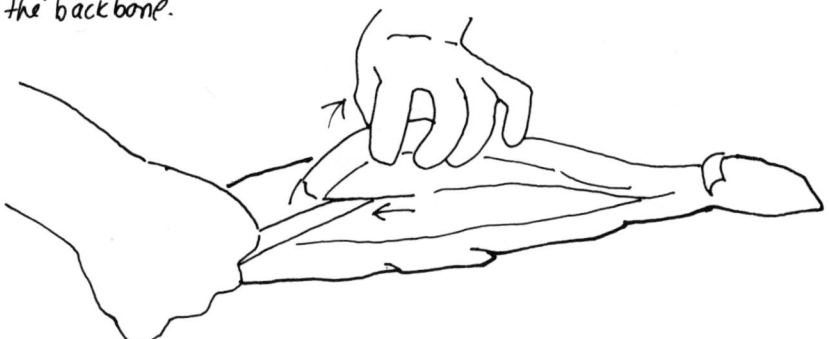

Striped bass can be used in most recipes and good fish cookbooks are filled with excellent recipes for cooking and serving bass. Here are two of my favorites that take advantage of the fish's good looks and taste. They are for fish from five to ten pounds and both demand a large oven and a large serving tray, because the fish will go in and come out whole, so it really looks like a striped bass on the table.

Baked Bass

Scale and clean a bass, leaving on the head, tail and all fins. Fill the gut cavity with any dressing you wish. I like chopped onions, sweet peppers, celery, bread crumbs, melted butter, salt and pepper. Place the fish on heavy aluminum foil that has been oiled, and brush the fish with oil on top. Add two strips of bacon, wrap the fish tightly in the foil, and place it on a baking sheet. Bake at 450 degrees for 20 minutes, then at 350 for another 40 minutes. Check to see if the meat is firm and white, not dry. Put the foil-wrapped fish on a large serving platter and open it at the table. Sniff once and dig in. Use small forks and your fingers—I really don't believe fish can be eaten without fingers.

Poached Bass, served cold

Borrow, rent, beg, steal, or buy a fish poacher big enough to hold a whole big bass. Start with a whole scaled gutted fish, with its head, tail and fins on. Wrap the fish in cheesecloth and ease it into the poacher filled with enough boiling salt water to cover the fish. Turn the heat down until the water just simmers and cook covered for 30 minutes. Take the fish out and, while still in the cheesecloth, wrap it tightly in aluminum foil and chill it (the foil keeps the fish moist). When serving time comes, unwrap the fish gently and serve it whole, garnished with whatever fresh vegetables are available. Served this way, striped bass is delicate and beautiful.

Notes
GOOD RECORDS MAKE FOR GOOD CATCHES.